THE OTHER FIVE SENSES

VINCENT TROPEPE

Copyright (c) Vincent Tropepe
All Rights Reserved
Published in The United States of America
Library of Congress Cataloging - in - Publication Data
Tropepe, Vincent A- 1st EdiThe Other Five Senses: subtitle here—
Understanding The Art Of Hospitality

I. Culinary Arts
II. Career Development
III. Hospitality Industry

Printed in The United States of America
10 9 8 7 6 5 4 3 2 1
1st Edition

THE OTHER FIVE SENSES

DEDICATION

With much love, respect, and admiration I would like to dedicate this book to...

Geraldine Austin
Rocco Coluccio Jr.
Anna D'Angelo
Mario Fico
Dave Greco
Onica Isaacs
Daniele Kucera
Seymone Moodley
Jonathan Nunez
Robert Oliver Jr.
Charlene Powery
Andrew Quinzi
Marco Pierre White
Mary Stella Zdeb

A NOTE FROM CHEF

Hello Everyone!

I want to take this moment to express how grateful I am to have another literary work of mine published. I feel so overwhelmed by the continued loyal growing readership of my work. This book is far different than the rest. It is both the blueprint of what I call 'the other five senses' for those who want to have a strong culinary career as well as gives tremendous insight to what it takes to provide an exceptional dining experience that the public demands from chefs and restaurants so this book serves both the industry and the dining public.

I hope that this work both educates and brings a newfound awareness to The Other Five Senses: Understanding The Art of Hospitality.

Other Books By Chef Vincent Tropepe Include

In My Whites
A Matter of Culinary Perspective

SLAUGHTERED
How Inconsistent Lockdowns Collapsed The Hospitality Industry During COVID-19

Roasted, Chopped & Beaten
When Cities Declare War On The Restaurants That Feed Them

ROOTS
Unlocking The Potential & Discovering The Delicious In All Natural Ingredients

Table of Contents

Preface
1

Chapter One: The Original Five Senses of the Human Body
3

Chapter Two: A Sense of Hospitality
51

Chapter Three: A Sense of Self and Culinary Identity
78

Chapter Four: A Sense of Timing
128

Chapter Five: A Sense of D.F.C (Discipline, Focus & Consistency)
164

Chapter Six: A Sense of Humor
200

My Final Thoughts
233

Preface

As I reflect on a twenty-year culinary career, I see where I started how my techniques, skills, perspective and approach have evolved and how it has become more and more fine-tuned. I view and study the many variables that not just shaped the hospitality landscape, but also society.

By default there are many factors that affect society (too many to write about in this work), and those factors shape the viewpoints of society and without a doubt also affect the people of society's choices and affect industries and the hospitality industry is one of them.

In this work, I skillfully articulate *the other five senses* needed that cooks and chefs and really any person holding a position in the hospitality industry must possess in order for the public to have an exceptional experience. For restaurants many might be surprised that it goes far beyond the chopping, mincing, deep frying and grilling and other preparation, cooking and baking techniques.

There are many reasons I'd like to explain why a work like this is so important – in fact even critical to be read by the dining public as well as those aspiring to be a culinary professional in the future. If I were to write about all of the reasons in this preface that alone would be a book within itself, but I will explain a few reasons here briefly. Unfortunately, social media influencers who are opinion based have diluted the craft of being a chef. These "influencers" who have no culinary background, the high probability to not be able to cook or bake the very items they criticize or give a score to are more interested in being the next viral sensation at the cost of a real culinary professionals. If a patron for whatever reason did not like something the respectful thing to do is return it and ask for something else, but influencers take no thought that a TikTok video or Instagram post can easily undo years of professional development and investments. I believe that receiving criticism is healthy and that it helps develop ones craft. There is responsibility that comes with having an audience, and the way influencers behave today they don't understand that responsibility.

The hospitality industry has also seen actors and singers all of a sudden take part in saturating the market with even more white noise, but what is even worse the hospitality industry as also seen chefs make desperate money grab business moves because of a built in audience. From selling subpar slices of cake in vending machines to another hot head chef who embarrasses people on national television about not using fresh ingredients, but yet releases a line of frozen dinners that I would not even serve to a Cocker Spaniel. Sure everyone has their reasons and rationale for doing what they do, but in the performance of those actions it not only causes public confusion, but it makes the craft of being a chef tarnished and discounted. It causes a blemish on the idea of what a chef is. And clearly even these seasoned chefs need to fine tune their *other five senses* as well.

With that being said, I'm very proud of *The Other Five Senses: Understanding The Art of Hospitality*. This is an honest look for the dining public, foodies and aspiring culinary professionals to examine the qualities and *other senses* needed to accurately, consistently, develop and execute the service and menu mix with the highest obtainable standards that the public deserves and for the culinary professionals and culinary community to have a blueprint for sustainable success.

CHAPTER ONE

The Original Five Senses of the Human Body

Human beings incredible marvels of evolution, and complex design, have an amazing sensory system that allows us to navigate and interact in the environment around us. In the center of it all are our five senses of origin, which include sight, hearing smell, taste, and touch. Each one of them provides the unique ability to experience external stimuli, which transform these into meaningful experiences. Before we discuss the *other five senses*, let's dive into the fascinating world of these five essential senses by exploring their mechanism as well as the importance and role they play in everyday life.

Vision is without doubt among the top important human senses, and plays an essential role in the way we see and perceive our surroundings. The sight is responsible for the majority of external stimuli that we see the most important source for understanding the world around us - and being the most fundamental part of this complex process: Our eyes is an incredible feat of bioengineering.

The anatomy of the eye is comprised of a number of important structures that play a role in the ability of seeing. The cornea is the main entry point for light. Begins first, and its curvature assists in directing the light's rays onto certain areas within it. It is behind it that lies the ameba-like substance that further reflects light, while also maintaining intraocular pressure, and ensuring that vision remains clear.

Light is directed towards the pupil, which is an adjustable aperture in the middle of the eye's colored portion called an iris through which light is able to enter and departs through an adjustable pupil-sized hole at the center of the iris. The pupil expands or dilates, it regulates the amount of light that enters your eye, maximizing your vision in various lighting conditions, and shielding the inner eye from being exposed to too bright light sources is possible.

When light hits the lens, which is a flexible and transparent structure allows it to adjust the focus of light, it is surrounded by accommodation that alters its shape in order to ensure that light rays are focused precisely on the retina. Accommodation lets us quickly concentrate on objects at different distances, by changing its shape in accordance with the distance is a crucial process to shift focus between objects with different distances. The retina, which is located behind each eye, is made up of cells that are sensitive to light and transform sunlight into signals that allow vision. The real magic is in the retina!

The retina is home to millions of photoreceptor cells referred to as cones and rods. They transform sunlight into signals the brain is able to comprehend. Rods are larger and extremely responsive to light which allows us to see in dim lighting conditions better than cones, however because they lack color separation, they create black and white images in dim lighting conditions.

Cones perform best in bright lighting conditions and are essential to discerning details and color in more fine areas. Humans usually have three kinds of cones that correspond to different wavelengths of light, such as green, red, and blue hues. The brain uses the data from the cones in order to produce every possible shade that is which are interpreted as hues. Cones and rods work seamlessly, allowing us be able to experience every type of visual sensations ranging from the tiniest of glimmers in dark as well as rich, detailed images in bright environments, up to dimly lit scenes with virtually no illumination.

Once photoreceptors transform sunlight into electrical signals they transmit these signals straight to brain through the optic nerve, which is comprised of million of nerve fibers which transmit information from your brain's visual cortex. The journey begins in the optic nerve where nerve fibers cross over and processing the visual information of each eye of both brain hemispheres. This crossing is essential for depth perception as well as binocular vision, which allows one to see three-dimensional depth as well as distance perception.

The visual cortex located in the occipital region of the brain converts electric signals to create visual pictures. This brain region is specialized in processing different aspects of vision like the color, brightness, shape and motion.

Our eyesight plays an essential part in shaping our perception about the environment around us and how we behave within it. With eyesight, we are able to see the faces of others, can read and take in the beauty of nature and can navigate our environment easily. In addition, visual cues play an a crucial role in non-verbal communication, such as understanding body language and facial expressions. The sight also plays a crucial part within our brain functions, as well as recall and memory processes. Visual learning is among the most effective methods of learning. Visual imagery helps to preserve and recall memories faster than any other method.

Human eyes are able to perceive a wide range of colours. The ability to perceive colors is based on our brain's interpretation of the interactions between different cone types when exposed to different wavelengths of light. Individual differences may also affect their perception because of different numbers and locations of cones inside their retinas. Human vision extends beyond color recognition, encompassing subtle changes in contrast and brightness that enable us to discern patterns, textures and even details more quickly. Additionally, our ability to sense motion allows us to react quickly on changes that occur in the surroundings.

Although the visual system might be able to withstand the pressure, it is susceptible to problems. Commonly, visual impairments are myopia (nearsightedness) as well as hyperopia (farsightedness) astigmatism (distorted vision) as well as presbyopia (an age-related problem in focus on objects in close proximity). The more serious conditions such as glaucoma cataracts, macular degeneration, and glaucoma could cause severe sight loss or blindness. The effects of eye disorders go beyond just impairing your vision. they can seriously impact levels of living as well as independence and the ability to carry out every day tasks. So, it is imperative to have regular eye exams and proper care should be offered to ensure the health of the eyes.

Since the beginning of time, our eyes have changed to accommodate changing requirements and conditions, changing in accordance with the environment. The latest advancements in medical science continue to enhance our understanding of problems with vision like corrective lenses, laser eye surgery, and retinal implants that have brought significant improvements for people with visual impairments. Genetics research is advancing rapidly stem cell therapy, genetics and artificial intelligence potential for breakthroughs that could be able to treat or even eliminate blindness and other severe vision disorders.

Our eyes, which are our windows into the universe, is a remarkable aspect of our senses and appreciation. In addition, it allows us to recognize and appreciate the beauty of the world that surrounds us, but it is vital for survival as well as communication and cognition. Through a deeper exploration of the capacities and the depths of human vision, we gain more insight into the profound impact it has on our daily lives.

Hearing, which is one of the most important senses in human existence allows us to have the ability to hear sound waves that travel through the air. They are then captured by the ear - an organ specifically built to receive auditory perception before being processed by our auditory systems into the sounds that we hear and interpret from our everyday surroundings. The ear is a tripartite auditory organ Our ears are marvels of biology engineering. It is comprised of three parts: the outer the ear, the middle ear and the inner ear, each part is a key component in hearing functions.

The outer ear is comprised of two main parts which include the pinna (visible part of the ear) and the ear canal. The pinna functions as a funnel that collects sound waves from the environment and redirect them into the ear canal, where they will be amplified before they are sent into your ear canal to process. This particular structure was designed to capture and concentrate the sound waves while amplifying their intensity before directing it towards the ear canal inside your ear.

The Other Five Senses

The end of the ear canal, there is an eardrum which is vibrating when it hears sound. The vibrations travel through the membrane that leads to the middle ear, which is comprised of three tiny bones referred to as the malleus, the incus and stapes, which function as connections between the eardrum as well as the inner ear. They amplify vibrations when they travel. They act as mechanical levers, intensifying vibrations that are then transmitted to the inner ear.

The ear's inner part is home to the cochlea, which is an organ with a snail shape, filled with fluid which is the center for sound transmission. Within this organ are a multitude of tiny hair cells that respond to various sounds that produce waves within its fluid medium, which alter hair cells mechanically once the sound waves reach them; These waves transform mechanical motion into electrical signals that then traverse the auditory nerve until they be received by your brain through your auditory nerve.

The auditory nerve, which is made by nerve fibers, transmits electrochemical signals to the cochlea the brain to process in the auditory pathways to hearing. The brain then interprets these signals and enables us to detect different sounds by recognizing both their origin and direction - crucial skills that are essential to be able to perceive spatial space and locate. Sound Perception The ability to discern the sound spectrum is diverse; not only are we able of hearing sounds, but we also have the ability to distinguish the various aspects of sound:

The pitch is determined by frequencies of sound. This lets us know if an audio is either high or low in pitch. This is an important element of the hearing system that can allow for enjoyment of music as well as speech understanding. Sound waves are of various amplitudes which determine their volume. Our ears are able to detect an amazing range of sounds which range from a soft whisper to the jet engine roar.

Timbre is a quality of sound that provides it with its distinct texture. It also helps us distinguish between sources that have similar levels of loudness and pitch. For instance, violins or piano with the same pitch sound differently.

Hearing is a vital component of speech communication. We depend on hearing to interpret and perceive speech, which allows for the exchange of thoughts, emotions as well as information. Hearing and being able to understand language is essential to personal development as well as education and social involvement.

Hearing is a crucial element in assessing the situation and ensuring safety. It helps us be aware about dangers that could be a threat, for example honks from the car horn and fire alarms, or a person calling out. Hearing can also help us be more secure in our surroundings while able to respond to situations in our surroundings more efficiently. Sound has a remarkable emotional power to trigger memories as well as stir emotions, and creates the stage. Music can boost our spirits, while rain drops soothe us. Having someone we love can be comforting. Our emotional response to music is one of the most distinctive features.

The hearing abilities of our bodies change through our lives. Infants react to sound, kids develop how to speak through listening and adults rely on hearing to communicate and socialization. Hearing loss can be a problem as we age, affecting the quality of life and communication, which is why taking care to protect it and seeking treatments for hearing loss, is essential.

The Other Five Senses

Hearing loss as a result of age hearing loss, noise exposure or other causes can seriously impact your communication and overall wellbeing. Modern medicine has a variety of solutions, from hearing aids, to implants for cochlear which can reduce the impact of hearing loss and improve life quality.

Research in the field of auditory science continues to uncover the secrets of hearing. Researchers are studying the way that sounds travel to our ears and the neural processes that are involved in hearing, and are pursuing innovative treatments for hearing loss and deeper insights into the auditory world.

Hearing is an amazing and essential sensation that connects us with the world in a profound way. Hearing is a crucial connection for safety, communication emotional, and enriching experiences. It opens up doors, generates memories and makes life more enjoyable! Understanding its intricate nature, we gain a deeper understanding of our body's architecture when we interact with the world around us. By securing and focusing on this vital sense, we are able to fully enjoy all the auditory experiences that await us!

A taste (gestation) can be described as an essential element of our lives that is interwoven into every day life and in the culture. The tongue is the center of this sensory journey because it is covered in taste buds, which are tiny but powerful sensory devices that allow us to experience an endless variety of flavors.

Taste buds are an extremely microscopic structure that houses receptor cells that are tuned to five primary flavors: salty, sweet, sour bitter, and umami. Sweetness is typically a sign of energy-rich foods such as carbohydrates. The sourness is a sign of acidic compounds that are that are found in food items, but often a sign of spoilage or fermentation, it gives a freshness and zing for our dishes. Saltiness is a crucial factor for maintaining the bodily processes. It can also enhance flavors, and bitterness brings balance and complexity to the food, while umami the fifth flavor, indicates the presence of amino acids and nucleotides that are found in protein-rich food items.

The interaction of food particles with receptor cells trigger a series of biochemical processes that culminate in electrical signals being transmitted into the cortex of gustatory of the brain and decoded as taste sensations that are perceived. Taste is closely linked to other senses. Its experience is profoundly shaped by the smell. Olfaction plays a vital role in the perception of flavor and aroma molecules that are produced by food contribute greater than ever before to its overall character than the flavoring ingredients themselves are able to do.

Temperature and texture play vital factors in our experience of gestation. Food texture, whether it's soft, creamy, or fibrous - can add new levels of flavor. Temperature affects both the flavor intensity and the quality of flavors such as when you taste cold ice cream and warm soup. Taste is closely tied to diet and nutrition, which is the main driver in the choice of food and eating patterns. The evolution of taste was crucial to the survival of early humans by guiding them towards food items that were nutritious and preventing potentially harmful substances from being consumed.

Taste is a major element in the way we eat in the modern age and offers a wide range of options for food. However, it can also present challenges, as our natural inclination to sweet and salty flavours can result in unhealthy eating patterns and lead to unhealthy eating habits. Understanding our own tastes while observing nutritional and diverse food requirements is essential to ensuring health and well-being.

Taste is intrinsically linked to tradition and identity because its food practices are a reflection of the available ingredients and preference for taste across different cultures around the world. In everything from South Asian curries to Japanese umami flavours, taste is a key element in the culinary landscapes of a region. Rituals and celebrations in cultural ceremonies and celebrations often focus on certain food items and tastes, thereby granting them with more importance than just providing food. The taste of food is a way to tell stories of the past and strengthen bonds with the community.

Psychological aspects of Taste Taste psychology are an interdisciplinary field that investigates how emotional and mental aspects affect our perception of taste. Our preferences for taste may be influenced by events and memories or the mood. Comfort food items often are a source of pleasant memories, with warmth and emotions which bring back memories and may trigger memories of warmth or nostalgia. The presentation of food and the setting affect a lot the taste of food. For instance, a tastefully placed meal in a beautiful setting can be more delicious and aromatic when served in a less appealing manner.

Disorders of the Taste and Their Impact Disorders and their Impact problems, such as the ageusia (loss in taste) and dysgeusia (distorted taste) could have severe adverse effects on health and quality of life. The reasons for these ailments can be due to illness, medication or simply getting older and resulting in a decreased appetite and a poor diet - which is a sign of their importance to general health.

Scientists continue to unravel the complexity of tasting. Recent research has focused on the genetics that influence tastes and sensitivities. In addition, there is increasing curiosity about how taste receptors are used outside of in the gustatory system for instance in appetite regulation or metabolism regulation.

Future of flavor presents amazing possibilities at the intersection of health and gastronomy. Food scientists and chefs alike are exploring innovative ways to make delicious yet healthy dishes with natural ingredients that increase the taste without resorting to overly high salts or sugars. Flavor profiling and taste modulation technology is opening up new horizons in food production and catering to individual dietary requirements and preferences.

The sense of taste in all its countless varieties, transcends the simply sensory experiences it comes from a complex interaction between biology, culture and psychology that determines our relationship to food, impacts the health of our bodies and is an integral part of our social and cultural interactions. When we explore its nuances and depths, we are able to gain a deeper understanding of this amazing sense of taste and its significance within the human experience.

Olfaction, also known as smell is an integral and frequently overlooked aspect of the human experience. Our sense of smell can connect directly to emotions and memories frequently triggering powerful responses when we are exposed to just one smell. The biological system that we have called the olfactory sense detects and interprets a variety of smells. Inside the nasal cavity, there is an organ known as the olfactory epithelium, which contains millions of receptors designed to recognize different scent molecules. If an odor molecule bonds to any of the receptors the signal travels through the olfactory nerve until it reaches the bulb and stimulating additional senses.

The olfactory bulbs function as a processing centre which is where smell signals are interpreted and sent to various parts of the brain, including the limbic system which is composed of areas like amygdala as well as the hippocampus, which play a crucial role in memory and emotion processes which makes this link between limbic and smell systems the most important factor in creating emotional and emotional responses to scents.

Smell is an essential component of our mood and capacity to recollect memories. One scent can take us back to a past the past, triggering memories that we believed had long disappeared. This is that is known as The Proustian memory effect. It demonstrates how powerful an effect scent has on recall, typically, it triggers emotions that are more vivid and vivid over other stimuli.

The strong connection between the senses and emotions is evident in our responses to different smells. Certain scents are able to instantly soothe our senses - such as lavender's calming scent, for instance - and others, like smoke, warn us to danger. The emotional response we have to various scents isn't just mental in origin, but has roots that are deep in evolutionary history, where sensory perception was an integral part of the survival of.

One of the most enjoyable aspects of smell is its contribution to the enjoyment of food. A lot of people believe that taste alone controls the perception of flavor. actually the two combine to create all the tastes. This explains the reason that when the ability to smell is impaired because of illness, such as colds and other respiratory illnesses food might taste stale or bland. Aroma is a crucial element of the enjoyment of food. Freshly cooked breads or spices could profoundly influence our perception of its flavor, enhancing our appetites and making us more satisfied while eating. Chefs use this combination of taste and aroma in making dishes that do more than satisfy, but also add a new dimension to the dining experience.

Beyond its effects on taste and memory, our sense of smell also plays an important function as a warning system that alerts us to the possibility of dangers within our surroundings, such as gas leaks, food spoilage or smoke, making an important statement about the significance of smell in the evolution of humankind.

The way we perceive smell is a fascinating area of research and study. Every olfactory receptor on our noses has been programmed to detect certain molecular characteristics of odorants. When an odorant is able to bind with a particular receptor, a neuronal reaction is activated that relays information to our brain through intricate interactions between proteins, genes as well as neural networks. Our noses are incredibly sensitive and have the capacity to discern an immense number of scents which is estimated at trillions because of the number of genes that are dedicated to olfactory receptors. This makes the sense we have of scent among the most diverse senses genetically.

Our sense of smell doesn't rely solely on biological processes. Its perception can also be influenced by psychological and cultural factors. Different cultures can have different opinions about certain smells, which manifest in the form of food practices, the use of fragrance or social norms. Psychologically speaking, smells are able to affect your mood and behavior and even our interpersonal relationships. Studies have shown that certain scents can boost alertness, ease anxiety, or even promote sleep. Personal differences

The Other Five Senses

in the perception of smell could alter preferences for foods, scents, and even environments.

Odor disorders can have a hugely negative impact on the quality of life. A condition such as the anosmia (loss in sense of smell) as well as hyposmia (reduced capacity to smell) can have negative consequences for eating pleasure security, personal safety, and overall health. These disorders can be caused by the obstruction of nasal passages or neurological disorders or aging-related deterioration. anosmia may even be an early sign of certain neurological conditions, so its detection is crucial.

Enhancing the senses of smell requires different methods. Beware of harmful substances that could be harmful to olfactory receptors for example, chemicals and pollutants are crucial. Engaging in activities that activate the senses - such as gardening or cooking - could aid in preserving it. Scent plays a crucial role in our lives every day that ranges from enhancing the pleasure of eating and serving to act as an alarm system. Its link to emotional and mnemonic processes reveals its richness and depth and as we continue to explore and comprehend olfaction, we gain an understanding of its function and are able to be able to experience the human sense with its various layers and complexities.

Touch is the basis of our human experience and interaction with the environment It provides a quick and direct connection to everything that surrounds us. The skin is the main source through which this sensation is experienced. The layers of skin are a collection of receptors that respond to temperature, pressure and pain.

Our skin performs multiple functions; it's an intricate sensory organ containing receptors and nerve endings which are skilled at detecting various forms of sensory stimuli like mechanoreceptors, which detect vibrations, or pressure thermoreceptors detect changes in temperature; nociceptors sense painful stimuli. Each is a key component in helping us comprehend the physical reality.

The mechanism of touch begins in the skin, and then travels through an intricate neurological path. When we are in touch with physical stimulus, these stimulate touch receptors, they transform this energy into electrical signals which are transmitted through peripheral nerves to the somatosensory cortex of our brains where they are interpreted to produce different sensations.

Touch is an incredibly multi-dimensional experience. It is possible to differentiate surface textures that range from soft and silky to rough sandpaperiness. We can also measure the object's weight and shape precisely to manipulate them and safely; identify the temperature variations from warm sun days to cold winter winds and determine the weight of objects that we are holding within our fingers.

The feeling of pain can be an effective warning system that alerts us to the possibility of dangers, and prompting us to avoid things like extreme heat as well as sharp items that may be harmful. The perception of pain can differ based on both psychological and physical elements; however, it is true that pain perception plays an essential role in preventing injury as well as aiding healing processes.

Touch is crucial for human development and emotional bonding starting from infancy to. The stimulation of the tactile sense plays

The Other Five Senses

an important part in the development of physical, mental and social development. The softness of a gentle touch can soothe infants to show its significant impact on the human bond and well-being.

Touch remains a crucial element in adult friendships. Touch can convey a variety of emotions, from affection expressed through a hug, to comfort expressed through gentle pats on the back creating opportunities to strengthen relationships as well as build trust and bonds that last between individuals.

In everyday life, tactile input is essential to perform a myriad of activities including typing, writing and threading needles to doing intricate tasks like the work of craftsmen. The skills they acquire through touch enhance their capacity to create repairs, create and heal quickly and accurately. Professionals such as craftsmen surgeons, and artists depend heavily on their hands as a component of their work. Professionals like craftsmen rely on touch in order to carry out intricate tasks with precision and efficiency.

Our sense of touch isn't only a part of us; it also works with other senses to create an accurate perception of the world. Multisensory integration takes place in the brain and can enhance food experiences - not solely based on taste, but that includes aroma perception, texture perception and visual appeal perception. many more! For example, enjoyment of food involves more than just tasting, but also involving perception of texture through the sense of touch, smell through scent as well as visual appeal through visual appeal and sight. Interplay between our senses gives depth and depth to our experiences and makes them more memorable and meaningful. Additionally, they play a vital part in our survival by helping us quickly recognize the changes happening in our environment and react effectively.

Recent technological advancements attempts to recreate the sensation of touch have led to systems that rely on haptics for feedback ranging from virtual reality experiences to remote-operated surgical instruments - that utilize it for improved user experience and accuracy. Being able to replicate the sensation of touch electronically can open up new avenues for interaction between human and computer gaming, medical, and gaming technology.

Touch can also be beneficial in therapeutic environments. Techniques like massage therapy make use of the ability to reduce stress, ease discomfort and encourage healing and relaxation. It also provides both psychological and physiological advantages in health and wellness environments alike.

While touch is a vital sense, it's not immune from diseases that hinder its ability to function. Disorders like neuropathy - which can affect nerve function - could result in a loss or alteration of sense of touch and sensory issues. These can seriously affect the living quality by making daily tasks more difficult or reducing an individual's ability to comprehend their environment completely.

The tactile system is vital to our overall health. Regularly checking-ups, precautions and a healthy lifestyle can all assist in maintaining and protect the sense of touch as well as being conscious of changes in our the sensitivity of our fingers that could indicate the beginning of health issues.

The advancements in research on tactile perception continue to improve the understanding we have of this sensation. The future research will shed understanding of its complexity, neuronal pathways that impact the human mind and behavior and may provide new solutions for disorders of the tactile sense or improved sensory experiences using technology.

Touch is an integral part of our experience. It is essential to our interaction with the physical world and for establishing connections with others. Touch affects our perception, ensures our health, and enhances our the quality of our lives. As we get more familiar with and discover its depths and understanding the incredible capabilities of human bodies as well as how they interact with the world around them. Touch is an evidence of the complexity of human perception while highlighting its multiple dimensions which makes touch even more intriguing!

Health of the senses can be neglected yet is essential for our overall health. The senses we have - vision hearing, taste smell, and touch contribute to the way we live our lives. They help us connect to the world around us, impact interactions between people, influence our perceptions of the world in our environment, and boost the quality of our lives overall. The health of these individuals is of the utmost importance because impairments could negatively impact our everyday activities such as social interactions, or even mental wellbeing.

One of the most important aspects for maintaining a healthy sense of smell is to ensure regular health checks. Regular examinations are essential for early detection and treatment of any potential problems, for example examinations of the eyes that identify conditions such as cataracts, glaucoma or macular degeneration prior to them causing cause serious damage. Hearing tests can detect the early loss of hearing, so prompt intervention can be made and dental exams ensure that your taste remains in top condition, while regular physicals identify issues that are related to smell or touch.

Diet, exercise and abstaining from unhealthy habits are essential to keeping the sensory system in good condition. Physical and nutritional exercise are among the key components needed to keep your senses in good condition. They are all essential to the ideal lifestyle plan for healthy living:

Diet: To ensure optimal health in the senses eating a diet high in vital minerals and vitamins such as omega-3 fats vitamin A C and zinc are essential. Omega-3 fatty acids, C & Z also help to improve eye health. antioxidants could help protect against aging-related loss of sensory. Regular exercise can boost the flow of blood, and this aids in maintaining the well-being of the sensory organs, such as ears and eyes.

Beware of harmful habits Avoid harmful habits: Smoking and alcohol consumption can have a devastating impact for the health of your sensory organs. Smoking can increase the chance of developing cataracts and macular degeneration due to age, and drinking excessively can affect your nervous system which can affect the perception of smell and taste. Security Measures to Protect Sensory Health It's critically essential that our senses be protected from environmental hazards and taking measures to protect the senses against environmental dangers is essential.

Eyesight: Wearing sunglasses to protect the eyes against UV radiation and making sure we have the right lighting is vital to protect our eyesight from damage caused by sunlight and a proper lighting is vital to prevent eye strain. To protect your hearing, wearing earplugs or headphones that block noise for prolonged exposure to loud sounds can protect your the ears from hearing loss caused by noise and help ensure that their hearing is free of damage.

Smell and Taste: avoiding harmful chemicals and pollutants that may harm the smell and taste receptors is essential.

Contact: Wearing protective equipment such as gloves when in hazardous areas will protect your nerve endings and skin from harm that could occur.

Being aware of changes in the sensory capabilities is essential. Sensory impairments that are early indicators could include difficulties focusing or hearing loud sounds in a distorted manner or changes in taste/odor along with decreased sensitivities to touch. These may all be indicators of health conditions such as neurologic disorders, diabetes or infections, and must be notified of medical attention immediately.

Sensory impairments can have significant psychological effects, such as depression, social withdrawal and anxiety. Hearing loss can lead to the feeling of being isolated from others, while vision impairment may reduce the independence of a person. It is essential to recognize these effects for coping with sensory loss effectively.

The technological advancements have led to numerous aids to enhance the sensory function of the body:

- Hearing aids and Cochlear Implants Hearing aids and Cochlear Implants: These devices are able to significantly enhance hearing for people with hearing loss.
- Vision Aids: from glasses to contacts lenses to laser procedures, many options are available for correcting vision issues.

- Tactile Aids: For those who have difficulty using their hands, devices such as feedback based on vibration devices could provide needed support in everyday tasks.

Rehabilitation therapy can help those who are struggling with sensory impairment, enhancing their everyday activities and enhancing the quality of their lives.

Knowledge is power, so the process of educating yourself and seeking community support are essential elements of managing your sensory health. Being a part of support groups, participating in local programs and staying up-to-date with medical advances offer valuable assistance and sources.

Sensory well-being and mental health are intimately linked; prolonged stress can lead to a worsening of problems with sensory perception, while impairments in sensory processing can cause mental health issues. Counseling methods for stress management or mindfulness to improving mental health can be beneficial to overall well being.

The health concerns related to sensory perception vary greatly throughout life:

- For children: It's vital that sensory issues be detected early to ensure optimal development in children. Regular visits to the pediatric doctor will facilitate prompt intervention should any issues with sensory development arise.
- Adults: It's vital for adults to be alert to lifestyle influences and exposures to the environment that could affect the health of their sensory system.
- Seniors: As sensory functions declining as we age, seniors require regular check-ups, and perhaps adaptive technology

or devices to assist in the preservation of the sensory function.

Environmental factors, including pollution and health issues around the world, could affect the health of your eyes. Screen time can contribute to strain on the eyes and vision issues. Taking preventive measures such as frequent breaks from screens as well as wearing eye protection is essential in reducing the risk.

The importance of healthful sensory perception cannot be overstated. The senses are at heart of our lives and ensuring their well-being is crucial to living a full, enjoyable life. Through regular health checks as well as a healthy lifestyle, security actions and awareness programs, as well as technological support systems, we can ensure our senses are protected and still delight in the many experiences they bring throughout our lives.

The five senses that make up our human body which include hearing, sight the smell, taste, and even touch remarkable in terms of their complexity and the purpose they serve. As a window to the outside world they offer us essential information that informs our perceptions, experiences and interactions with people beyond us. Through exploring and understanding these senses, we can gain deeper understanding of their complex functions as well as the many ways that they connect us with the outside world.

Taste buds do not have an equally distributed area across the tongue, with specific regions being more sensitive to particular flavor than others. The traditional tongue maps have been proven false, as personal differences can greatly affect taste perception.

Sensitivity to taste and preferences are influenced through environmental and genetic influences some people are "supertasters" with an increased sensation of bitterness. In addition, environmental influences like the culture of the area and exposure to various food items as early as is possible are all crucial in determining tastes preferences.

The taste of food plays a significant role in influencing the choices we make regarding our diet and, therefore overall health and nutrition. For example, a preference for sweet or salty flavors could cause overeating in specific food categories, and possibly causing harm to health, while avoiding bitter flavors can reduce the consumption of vegetables - it's important to be aware of and controlling our preferences for taste to design a healthy eating plan.

The taste of food is a crucial defense against ingestion of hazardous chemicals, and bitter taste being particularly effective in deterring against food poisoning or spoilt and ensuring our survival through the evolution of humankind.

Taste is the foundation of all culinary art forms and cultures alike, playing a crucial part in the development of identities and traditions across the world. Regional cuisines develop in accordance with the available ingredients and the residents their personal preferences for taste; events and celebrations usually focus on food, which makes taste an integral part of the shared experience. Taste and other senses Taste is inextricably connected to other senses, specifically smell. Aromas play a major influence on our perception of taste, while the touch gives details about temperature and texture to enhance the sensation of trying something new.

The sensitivity to taste decreases with age, and this can adversely affect eating habits and nutrition intake in older people. This can be due to factors such as decreased the density of taste buds or changes the production of saliva. Troubles with Taste can severely affect living quality. Conditions like agedusia (loss of flavor) as well as dysgeusia (distorted taste) may be due to a variety of reasons such as medication-related reactions as well as neurological disorders or infections.

Enhancing taste sensitivity could require tiny steps, such as abstaining from smoking cigarettes, which may affect taste, and experimenting with various spices and flavors when cooking. A healthy mouth should be considered when determining how to improve the sensitivity of taste.

The study of gestation aims to expand our knowledge of how taste functions and the implications it has for nutritional and health. Research areas currently being studied include the relationship with taste as well as metabolic diseases and the creation synthetic taste receptors as well as manipulating taste perception in order to improve the quality of food.

The sense of taste is a complex and multi-dimensional sense that plays an vital roles when we interact with our surroundings around us, from our food choices to the enjoyment of life, all the way to safeguarding us from harmful substances. Maintaining and understanding the health of our digestive system is essential to our overall health when we delve deeper into the complexities of taste, we gain a deeper understanding of its function as the basis of survival, but also the unique role it plays in food as well as cultural environments.

Mechanism and Function Smell also known as olfaction is a vital element of human life that is often ignored. The body uses this sense to identify and interpret different chemicals that are that are floating around in the air. this process starts within the nasal cavity where the olfactory receptors sense scents in the air, also called odorants. When they recognize a scent and send signals to the brain, allowing us to detect a wide range of smells. Olfactory Receptors Olfactory Receptors are cells found inside the nose. They have the ability to recognize different scent molecules and bind to them, which in turn stimulates neural responses when one of the smell molecules is bound to these receptors.

Olfactory Bulb located beneath the frontal lobes of the brain, the olfactory bulb is the initial stop for processing olfactory data. When scent molecules trigger sensory receptors within the nasal cavity information regarding the scent is transmitted to this region of the brain. This is where the analysis and identification begin.

Perceiving smell is a complex process. It involves decoding intricate patterns generated by a variety of molecules of odor to recognize distinct smells. This is controlled by the olfactory bulb which is capable of discerning different smells. When this organ processes them the information it receives about them is sent to various regions of the brain which are responsible for processing emotions and memory.

The relationship between smell and memory One of the most fascinating features of smell is the close connection to memory. The olfactory bulb is connected to connections to the regions of the brain that deal with the processing of emotions and memory like amygdala and the hippocampus. These connections are the reason why certain smells trigger sensations or memories often referred to in"the "Proustian effects."

The Other Five Senses

Smell and taste are linked when it comes down to the sense of taste. Aroma plays a significant role in determining how we feel the taste of food. In fact having a weak sense of smell, for instance in the case of a cold, may make it difficult for one to appreciate food correctly. Flavor perception is a combination of both aspects of sensory input. comprehension is heavily influenced by the two experiences being in sync.

The perception of scent is vital for our survival, assisting us identify threats like flames, leaks of gas, and food loss. This is a legacy of evolution that means early humans relied heavily upon smell to stay away from toxic substances, or to alert them to threats to the environment.

Smell is a key element in sexual and social interactions. Body odors, which communicate biochemical information about an individual frequently play a major part in sexual attraction. Pheromones (which comprise certain chemical smells that trigger certain emotions in human beings) are able to play an indirect function as signalling for communication. They can also have a an enormous influence on sexual and social behavior; however, their exact role in human beings remains a subject of research.

Odor disorders range from the anosmia (the loss of the sense for scent) and hyperosmia (increased the sensitivity to smells). Both of these conditions can have significant effects on the quality of living, affecting eating pleasure, social interactions and safety. Anosmia can cause decreased intake and even nutritional deficiency and also a lack of ability to discern dangerous odors. Like many other sensory systems, our perception of smell diminishes with age, reducing the taste and the enjoyment of eating. Additionally its diminished capacity can pose the risk of a potential danger to our safety.

Odor is deeply ingrained into the daily routine and culture that range from religious rituals with incense, to choosing the right scents to use for personal purposes. The psychologically, smells affect behavior, mood and performance which is the reason for aromatherapy being an alternative to therapy.

Recent advances in technology and neuroscience have given researchers more understanding of the sensory system. Research is not only uncovering how we sense smells, there are also new methods being developed to treat smell problems as and digital scent technology advancement.

Our sense of smell, also known as smell, plays a crucial aspect of our daily lives. From eating food to interactions with people and memories the smell of olfaction plays an essential role. As we continue to uncover its mysteries, we gain an understanding of this incredible sense that affects our well-being and the survival of.

The term "touch" (tactile sense) is the ability to feel pressure or physical contact on the skin. It includes sensations like temperature, pressure or pain.

Sensory receptors are located across the skin and respond to various types of stimuli. Neural Pathways: The signals generated by these receptors are transmitted along neural pathways that traverse the nervous system, until they reach their destination, which is the brain.

Touch is a crucial aspect of the development of a person and their well-being and wellbeing, from the dexterous activities that call for dexterity social interactions that help build bonds and foster friendships. Additionally our sense of touch can warn us about environmental hazards by causing pain.

The Other Five Senses

Interplay of the Senses The five senses are not operating independently, but they frequently collaborate to create an overall view of our surroundings. This multisensory integration enriches our interaction with the world around us, enriching our experiences and assisting us to respond effectively to various situations.

The maintenance of our senses is essential for overall health and well-being, so regular health checks, a well-balanced diet, exercise, and precautionary measures (like the use of sunscreen and earplugs) can all aid in maintaining their health. Be aware of any changes to sensorimotor abilities could suggest health issues that need additional examination.

Sensory impairments or loss of sensory function can have a significant impact on a person's living quality, causing problems with mobility, communication and self-reliance. Rehabilitation and assistive technology can be used to mitigate its negative impacts.

The ongoing research is aimed at expanding our knowledge of our senses. The advancements in neuroscience and technology are promising in the development of new therapies for sensory disorders and providing enhanced sensory experiences like virtual reality, or better prosthetics.

Five senses that the foundation of our lives such as hearing, sight sense, taste, smell, and touch are vital in shaping our perception and interaction with the world around us, delivering essential functions for survival, communication, and enjoyment. Their importance cannot be understated and ensuring their health is crucial to living a happy and exciting life. As we gain knowledge about them, we gain a greater understanding of their complexity and the marvels that human eyes can see.

Culinary arts is a form of art that combines the five senses of hearing, sight and smell - all at once to create culinary masterpieces. This makes the role of a chef or cooks not just a job, but also a complete sensory experience. In the culinary arts, sight is a highly revered aspect. It is often the first impression of food when it is first encountered; creating the stage to ensure a pleasant dining experience. The phrase used by professional kitchens that "we have our eyes on the food first" is particularly relevant here and its visual appeal is not just a bonus feature but rather an essential element in overall enjoyment and perception of dishes served.

Chefs are aware that making visually appealing meals is similar to creating art works; it takes a keen eye to shape, color, and the composition. The way food is presented on the table can significantly impact the dining experience and satisfaction. A visually appealing platter that is bursting with vibrant colors and textures that creates anticipation for the flavors that are to follow!

Color is a major factor in the food's appeal. Vibrant hues are usually thought of as more fresh and delicious, which chefs make use of by making use of a variety of bright ingredients to make an appealing plate. For example, red tomatoes that are deep together with vibrant green basil leaves and delicious brown steak provide a memorable dining experience both visually as well as in terms of texture.

Form and arrangement on plates are vital elements for the visual appearance of food. Chefs use a variety of plating methods to improve the visually appealing dishes, ranging from arranging ingredients with care to ensure the balance and symmetry, to stacking or spreading techniques to create the height of and add depth. The aim is to design plates that look not only attractive but

The Other Five Senses

also tell a story through drawing the eyes of guests through all of the components of the dish's different elements.

Texture is an important factor in the visual appeal of every dish. The contrast of textures like the crispness from freshly cut lettuce and smooth sauces can create visual interest, and can enhance the dining experience. Chefs often use texture to bring layers of sophistication to their dishes and encourage diners to look around before eating!

Visual perception is a crucial element in plating as well as cooking. Being able judge the how fresh ingredients are an essential attribute for any chef. Freshness usually equates with quality of food. The most delicious dishes are made with the finest ingredients. A skilled eye can recognize subtle indicators of freshness like the bright hue of freshly picked vegetables or shiny, polished surface of fresh caught seafood, or the the firmness of high-quality cuts of meat.

The ability to see is essential in controlling how food is cooked, ranging from the caramelization of onions, or the cooking of meat to the rising of bread in the oven as an important indicator of how far the cooking process is progressing. The visual signals enable chefs to make rapid adjustments to the temperatures and time so that every element of the dish is cooked to the highest quality.

The kitchen's sight is a crucial aspect in ensuring safety and hygiene standards. Cleanliness and order is essential to ensure safe food preparation and chefs depend on their senses to detect possible hazards, such as spilled liquids that can cause cross-contamination or slipperiness among ingredients. A proper organization of equipment and ingredients also contributes to the safety and efficiency when cooking. The sight is an integral component of the culinary arts that extend beyond the kitchen. Lighting, decor, and table decor all contribute to an experience of dining that enhances the visual appeal of food. It is important to pay attention when arranging these elements to create a pleasant dining environment and experience.

The visual arts of culinary are multifaceted, combining art with practicality. Chefs depend on their eyesight as a crucial tool for making dishes that appeal to both the eyes and other senses. from the aesthetic presentation of food and ingredients to assessing the quality of the food and ensuring the safety of kitchens the eye plays a vital function in all aspects of cooking, creating expectations and shaping the experience that is to follow.

Hearing, particularly in an environment of professional kitchens is often overlooked but essential for cooks and chefs. The auditory cues that the kitchen go beyond the sound of background noise. They contribute to making culinary masterpieces, as well as ensuring seamless kitchen operations.

The sounds of the kitchen are as varied as the food they serve and each has its distinct rhythm and tone. One example is the sound of meat sizzling on the grill. This sound signifies Maillard Reaction that transforms the meat into delicious flavors. Its intensity and quality tells a cook whether to turn the grill or take it off the grill.

Like its look, stewing sauces and stews give you an auditory clue about the cooking process. A constant, soft bubbling sound signals that the dish is cooking at a suitable temperature. This allows flavors to mix and not burn or boil; however, loud or splattering sounding could signal to the chef that their temperature levels require adjustments. Knowing these clues will ensure your dish is perfectly

The Other Five Senses

cooked! Learning to interpret auditory signals will ensure that time and precision are maintained in the preparation of a dish!

Cutting vegetables or rubbing knives against a cutting board in a rhythmic manner and swiftly is a different orchestra in the kitchen, offering another proof of a cook's skill and efficiency with their knives. Chopping consistently is a sign of their systematic yet shrewd method of preparation vital for efficiency and safety in any kitchen.

Beyond the sound that cooks, the audio environment of the kitchen is the interplay between human interactions with machinery. The clanking of dishes and mixers whirring, as well as refrigeration units buzzing and hums from kitchen appliances create an auditory backdrop for cooking activity in kitchens. Although sounds that seem insignificant like these might seem unimportant to the general operation however, they are vital to keeping the flow and rhythm in every kitchen, whether it's signalling the completion of washing dishes, or the oven being in good condition or to maintain equipment!

Communication between kitchen staff is another aspect in which hearing is a crucial aspect. A busy kitchen demands vocal cues as well as calls and responses among staff members to help facilitate coordination so the ability to hear and process them swiftly is vital for expediting the flow of orders, managing workflow and ensuring the safety of your team. Chefs should be conscious of conversations in the midst of bustling kitchens to effectively manage their staff effectively.

The auditory cues that kitchens use aid in announcing chefs of emergencies like gas leaks, dropped knives and fire alarms which need immediate action and a prompt response from them. They are quick to respond, which ensures the safety of staff as well as the establishment from injuries that result from inadequate response from chefs. The kitchen's auditory experience can have a profound impact on the dining experience. The sounds coming from kitchens that are semi-open or open can increase the anticipation and enjoyment of their meal. pans and pots clanging as food cooks on grills, bustling kitchen noises, all of which help making dining an experience that is immersive for the patrons.

The kitchen's hearing is crucial to the kitchen staff and chefs as well as their own wellbeing. The excessive exposure to loud sounds could cause hearing loss So understanding and controlling its acoustics are essential components of a healthy lifestyle. This could include implementing noise reduction strategies and wearing hearing protection if needed and creating spaces that minimize the noise level.

Chefs utilize hearing as an essential tool to have in the arsenal of tools for cooking. Hearing is a complement to other senses, such as smell, taste and sight to enhance the cooking process and provide delicious culinary experiences, as well as efficient kitchen processes. Professional chefs are able to respond to kitchen sounds which not only enhance their food creations, but also helps ensure the safety of kitchen operations, playing an essential role in the science and art of food creation!

The sense of taste, within the context of culinary art is of major importance. It is the foundation of the reputation of every chef and their success the ability to discern how to balance and enhance flavors is what separates the ordinary culinary experiences from the most exquisite. While taste cannot be taught in a single moment the process of developing and enhancing it occurs over time through years of experience and continuous learning.

Cooking goes beyond making recipes and mixing ingredients It's an art form which requires understanding the flavors in order to create something more in comparison to its components. The palate of a chef is their most valuable advantage in knowing flavors. Their ability to recognize subtle flavors that create a dish can help create a harmonious balance of flavor whether making complex sauces or spiceing up their meats.

The taste is so delicate, minor adjustments in the ingredients or seasonings can profoundly alter its flavor, which requires the expertise of a skilled chef and a keen sense of taste when creating unforgettable dishes. Knowing the way flavor combinations interact with each other, the strengths or weaknesses, and the ways they can enhance or diminish by interacting with one another, as well as other sensory sensations like the smell and texture makes it possible for a chef to create delicious and memorable meals.

Taste is constantly evolving and is it is influenced by a myriad of aspects, such as the experiences of individuals and the cultural background of diners and chefs alike. Exposure to diverse food styles and ingredients from all over the world can dramatically increase a chef's repertoire of culinary skills and appreciation of flavor encouraging creativity and innovation at the kitchen table to create dishes that showcase a variety of diverse culinary traditions and methods.

Chefs learn and develop their palette by tasting and experimenting. Taste is an essential aspect of cooking. Chefs should test their food at different stages of preparation to make sure that the flavor develops according to expectations, and to adjust the seasoning or technique if needed. Also, exploring different ingredients and flavors can help broaden their palates; by stepping outside of your comfort zones, and stepping into unexplored culinary regions, they might discover delicious and surprising combinations!

Consistency is a crucial element of taste. Professional kitchens have to produce food that are consistent in flavor and quality in order to satisfy guests' expectations of eating food they've enjoyed previously they return to the restaurant. To achieve this consistency, they must use precise seasoning techniques, meticulous methods of preparation and an expert palate that is able to spot any flavor variations that occur.

Chefs need to not only create their own tastes but also be aware of their clients. This requires a thorough appreciation of tastes and trends in the food industry. Chefs need to balance their innovative vision with the needs of their patrons through minor adjustments that accommodate different palates without jeopardizing their cooking style.

Taste is closely linked with other sensory systems, including smell. Aroma can enhance the flavors of food items and a skilled chef is able to use this to benefit their customers. Additionally, the visual representation of food has an impact on the perceived flavor, further demonstrating the multisensory nature of cooking.

The trends and tastes of food change rapidly chefs must possess the flexibility and adaptability required to improve and develop their flavor. Constant learning, whether via reading, travel or a mentorship, or through trials and errors in the kitchen - is essential to their ongoing progress and achievement as chefs.

The Other Five Senses

The taste is the most important aspect of the culinary process. The ability to master it distinguishes a chef who is exceptional from a regular one. A perfectly tuned palette, developed through years of training and constant education, allows the chef to design meals that go beyond nutrition and turn into memorable experience. Taste is the hallmark of the best chefs. Their abilities to create a balance between flavors and developing without breaking any their consistency are truly amazing. The importance of taste is not only in culinary art, but it's the foundation of everything.

Aroma is an essential element of the culinary arts which defines flavor perception as well as the overall dining experience. This dynamic interaction reveals the depth and complexity of food creations. The importance of food is the palate and nose. Chefs' ability to discern and manipulate aromas is crucial to creating dishes that don't just taste great but also evocative and memorable, too. Aromatic food can create expectations, evoke emotions and transport diners to the past while can entice appetites and create anticipation for the delicious dishes.

Chefs frequently depend on their noses when choosing ingredients for their dishes. Aromas can give hints about the freshness, quality and nutritional value of the ingredients, for example the scent of fresh fruit and earthy mushrooms, or the salty smell of seafood could provide an indication of the freshness or quality of food. Similarly, the potency of herbs and spices can be assessed by their scent that lets chefs balance flavors and layer them efficiently.

Chefs who have experience know that how to mix herbs and spices to create captivating aromas is a skill to master, as chefs are aware of how aromas influences how we experience the taste of dishes. The attention they pay to details can be seen in the way they select and blend aromatic ingredients like spices, herbs and aromatic vegetables like celery, onions and garlic to create the base of their recipes creating complex aromas that enhance the flavor of a variety of meals.

The smell is an essential element of cooking. It helps chefs detect changes in the food they prepare as the process progresses, from onions that gradually change from sweet to sharp as they caramelize, to the smell of meat grilling over an open flame, or stew simmering on the stove. These are all indicators that guide chefs' decisions on the right time to alter the heat, stir or even include ingredients to ensure that each component of a dish is well completed.

The ability to spot subtle changes in the smell is vital to making sure that there are no mistakes. The smell of burning objects or the smell of food spoiling could cause a chef to be alert, allowing swift action to address any issues swiftly and in a safe manner. A acute nose is a vital tool for keeping quality and safety in creating food items.

In addition to the kitchen chef's olfactory talents are essential to making the perfect pairing of food and drink together. The interaction of aromas and flavors between food and drinks can enhance a meal and improve dining experiences by creating harmony between scents and flavors to take eating experiences up to new heights of enjoyment. Wines that are well-paired can enhance the flavors of dishes, while also adding notes that highlight certain features of them or providing additional sensory enjoyment altogether. Chefs collaborate with sommeliers in order to utilize their knowledge of aromas in order to create pairings that compliment each of the characteristics - like pairing earthy notes in the mushroom risotto, with strong aromas in pinot noirs for instance!

The Other Five Senses

Culinary art is about mastering aroma to serve and present dishes efficiently, with presentation having immense influence on the perceived smell. Freshly cooked food served straight from the stove can release an explosion of aroma that enhances the diners' excitement and appetite. In the same way adding fragrant garnishes or methods like smoking or infusing could enhance the olfactory appeal of a dish.

Smell is an integral component of dining and cooking which reflect the emotional and cultural contexts. Different cultures utilize different spices and herbs to create their unique cuisine These scents that evoke the place and traditions contribute to food being an integral part of cultural manifestation and celebration.

The smell is a key component of memories and emotions. Certain scents can trigger particular emotions or memories within people, which makes food an a powerful tool for telling stories and emotional bonding. The smell of a particular spice could trigger memories of cooking with grandma while a different dish could remind you of special events or memories of travel from the in the past.

Smell is a crucial but often overlooked aspect of culinary art. It plays a vital role throughout the cooking process, from choosing the ingredients, preparation, the pairing process and even serving. Knowing and manipulating the smells is essential to elevate an item from being healthy to an unforgettable multisensory experience for the diner; its ability goes beyond flavour enhancement to create bonds between food and diners as well as allowing chefs to express their artistic flair through food. That is the importance of it in contemporary food! It is important to understand that the sense of smell isn't just used by chefs to use tools, but rather as a means of expression in the world of culinary!

Touch in the culinary arts is a valuable and subtle skill which allows chefs to connect with their ingredients and dishes through touch, which creates an indelible conversation between the chef and the meal. Touch isn't just an act of cooking food items, but instead is an intricate dance the resistance to texture and suppleness that provides chefs with information about the condition and quality of their ingredients and food items.

Touch is a crucial element in cooking. When cooking meats, for example, chefs depend on their hands to determine their degree of doneness. The hardness of a steak and the firmness of chicken breasts, or giving in fish fillets are all excellent indicators of doneness that can't be observed with the eyes alone. Fingertip feedback or cooking utensils can tell that a cook if the food is at rare medium or well-done degrees. Mastery of this technique, which is often acquired through years of training is essential to create flawlessly cooked food items that have the best volume, flavor, and texture levels, while preserving all the essential qualities like moisture content, while also retaining moisture retention, as along with flavor flavors and textures.

Production of pastry and bread rely on the sense of touch to ensure their success as well. Bakers must have an acute sense of touch to assess dough's elastic properties, density and stickiness can provide information on the development of gluten as well as whether enough kneading is occurring. Then, the texture before baking as well as its change through baking, as well as the final crust/crumb depend heavily on this sense of touch and can result in perfectly baked bread loaves or flaky pastry!

The Other Five Senses

The ability to feel is a powerful tool in the selection of the best produce. From the firmness of fruits to the crispness of vegetables, as well as the turgor and flavor of herbs the tactile characteristics are indicators of quality and freshness. For instance, a firm tomato yields under pressure, whereas an overripe tomato has a soft feel; similarly, fresh cucumbers should have a the firm, hard exterior that gives easily when pressure is applied; similarly, a an examination of the tactile qualities can help select the best meat and fish products. Fresh meat and fish are those with firm textures that are able to bounce back when press and premium meats should exhibit some firmness when inspected closely The analysis of tactile characteristics also aids in deciding on the best meat and fish at market. Tactile analysis assists in determining these characteristics as indications of freshness and quality.

The ability to touch is crucial in the kitchen. Chefs need to be able to handle delicate ingredients such as herb or thin pastry sheets without harming them and also the ability required to make exact knife cutting, form ingredients according to their preferences and deal with a range of textures, ranging from hard to slippery to soft and ingredients. Touch is a crucial element of presentation and plating and presentation. The art of arranging food on a plate requires more than just visual abilities and a touch experience too. A chef should use the senses of their hands to create a balance between different textures, from smooth to crisp elements to create a memorable dining experience. Mixing soft textures with hard ones can add the depth and sophistication to the dining experience.

Chefs are heavily dependent upon their touch for keeping their kitchens safe. When they feel temperature via contact (often indirectly through utensils and oven gloves) chefs are able to gauge the temperature of their pans, grills or oven temperatures, food temperatures, and liquid temperatures that are vital to the cooking process and safety standards.

Touch is at the heart of culinary art; it creates a personal connection between the chef and the act of cooking in a profound and direct manner. With the help of touch, chefs can show their expertise as well as their care and attention to detail, while conveying their passion for the ingredients they transform into meals that provide more than food; they provide a sensory experience as well.

In an age that is increasingly driven by technology and automated the skills of a chef are still vital. While technology can replicate certain aspects of cooking but only human hands can bring the soul of food and create the most of an experience. It is also crucial for dining and cooking. Food prepared carefully and with care that engages the senses with its texture and mouthfeel becomes an element of dining and is just as important as its taste appearance and visual appeal. Cooking requires a precise balance between technical aspects such as temperature, texture, and doneness as well as artistic and individuality in the creations of food. Chef's skills combine the skills, knowledge and enthusiasm to create an integral aspect of the culinary arts.

It is a matter of assessing whether someone is able to thrive even when loss of one or two senses can be a test, which tests our endurance and ability to adapt as humans. Through time there have been numerous instances of people not just being able to deal with the loss of their senses but prospering and making significant contributions to the society despite it. While it is true that sensory loss can present problems, it could also be a path to incredible human potential and achievement.

The Other Five Senses

The key to the success of overcoming sensory loss is our brain's extraordinary ability to adapt. Neuroplasticity - or the ability to restructure itself by forming the new connections in our brains - play a crucial function. When the sense of a person is gone the other senses are often more powerful to compensate. For instance, people who are blind typically have an enhanced sense of smell, hearing and tactile senses that help them understand their surroundings more quickly. Stevie Wonder, born blind shortly after birth and an internationally recognized musician since shortly thereafter, has used this extraordinary ability to achieve extraordinary things. For instance his music has enthralled millions, not only because of his struggle to overcome handicap, but also because he utilized his enhanced sensory and auditory abilities to create timeless art that is a hit worldwide.

Deaf people benefit from a boost in sensitivities to tactile and visual, as was demonstrated through Helen Keller who was both blind and deaf; with assistance from Anne Sullivan's class, she was able to learn the sign language of tactile and became an accomplished writer, activist, lecturer and advocate for those disabled.

The success of those who suffer from sensory impairment is about changing the definition of success. The success of someone with sensory impairment may not be measured by standard standards but rather how they adapt and navigate their surroundings using different methods - maybe Braille literacy for those who are blind and the use of sign language by deaf people or other technologies and techniques that enable individuals to function more effectively in society and the surrounding environment.

Support systems play an integral part in the success of those suffering from sensory impairment. The support system can come in different forms, including family members and friends, educators and health professionals, as well as groups in the community can offer invaluable assistance and support that allows those who suffer from sensory impairments to live full and fulfilling lives.

Sensory impaired people typically have a unique perspective of the world that may inspire creativity and ingenuity. They might approach issues differently than those who are not with a tendency to find solutions that aren't immediately apparent in other areas. Their unique method of interpreting and communicating with the world is valuable in areas that span technology, science, arts, and business.

A psychological response to the loss of a sense is also essential. The process of navigating its different stages of grieve and acceptance requires a lot of resilience from human beings but being able to learn to accept and adapt to the loss of a sense could lead to personal growth and greater understanding of oneself and the world around us.

Opportunities for career and education for people with sensory impairments have made significant improvements over time due to legislation and growing societal acceptance of accessibility and inclusion. Workplaces and schools now regularly cater to their needs and provide essential tools and facilities that help them succeed.

The role models and representation of others cannot be undervalued, especially for people who suffer from sensory loss. Watching others who have faced similar challenges succeed can be an extremely motivating and inspiring experience, as well as creating a sense belonging and community. It also provides tangible proof that success is attainable. It is true that losing any one of the senses can present specific challenges, however it doesn't mean that you cannot succeed. Through adaptability, resilience help, and the use of other skills and techniques those who suffer from sensory impairments can lead full lives, despite physical limitations; their accomplishments are a evidence of the remarkable abilities of mankind and the endless potential that is in all of us.

There are examples of people who do not have any in the five senses, but who have had high levels of professional success within their areas of work.

Human accomplishment is awe-inspiring, with many people who have surpassed conventional limits and reached top of their fields despite overcoming formidable obstacles. Of all the challenges being unable to use one of the five senses is a remarkable example of human resilience and awe. In various periods of history people who are blind or hearing, smell or taste have overcome their handicaps to be successful in various fields and inspire generations of people by changing the perceptions of what was possible. This article highlights their accomplishments as well as imparting important lessons on the power of determination, flexibility and the endless possibilities of human thinking.

One of the most famous figures in history, Helen Keller was blind and deaf because of illness when she was a child however, she managed to achieve an internationally recognized writer, activist, lecturer and campaigner for the cause of disability rights and also inspiring people all over the world with her unwavering determination and awe-inspiring spirit.

Vincent Tropepe

Widely regarded as one of most outstanding composers in the world, Beethoven began losing his hearing in his late 20s and eventually becoming completely deaf. But, this didn't affect his work or leave a lasting impression on the history of music.

Blind since her twenties, Christine Ha started to loose her vision due to an auto-immune condition, Ha defied expectations by winning the third season of "MasterChef" in the United States. Her amazing palate and culinary abilities captivated viewers, while also demonstrating the strength of perseverance and aptitude when faced with challenges in life.

While losing his sight due epilepsy, John Bramblitt the artist discovered an extraordinary talent for drawing by using only his fingertips. Through the use of the use of raised lines and textures, his paintings are vibrant paintings which have gained his international recognition and proved that creativity has no limits.

The personal stories of those who have risen to the top of their careers despite having none from the five senses are an inspiring reminder of our ability to overcome, adaptability and innovation. All the way from Helen Keller to Jessica Cox These remarkable people have broken down stereotypes, overcame seemingly impossible obstacles and turned their handicaps into sources of inspiration and strength. Their achievements have not only redefined what it means to be successful but also highlight the endless possibilities of human potential. As we look back on their accomplishments and experiences, let us learn from their determination, courage and unwavering belief in the possibility of success Reaffirming our shared dedication to creating a society in which everyone, irrespective of their capabilities will be able to succeed and realize their ambitions.

The Other Five Senses

Cooking is usually viewed as a sensory experience that requires keen senses of smell, taste vision, and touching to prepare delicious meals. But there are extraordinary cooks who have defied the conventional expectations to create culinary excellence despite losing some or all of their senses. With a combination of ingenuity, determination and a profound love for their work they have overcome their handicaps and left an unmistakable mark on the culinary scene. This article explores the inspirational experiences of those who've conquered sensory hurdles and proved that culinary mastery knows no limits.

A celebrated chef from France, Jerome Henry lost his vision as a result of an eye degenerative disorder. In spite of this however, he never stopped pursuing his passion for cooking using his sense of smell, memory and tactile senses to make exquisite meals that enthralled critics and diners alike. With his unique method of cooking and his dedication to excellence Chef Henry has inspired numerous people who are disabled to pursue their culinary dreams around the world. His vision goes beyond the scope of vision.

Chef Norman Van Aken known for his expertise in French food Chef Norman had to lose his hearing early in his life due to a genetic disorder. Unfazed by the challenge Chef Norman honed his culinary skills with intense training and apprenticeships, relying on visual cues written communication, as well as tactile feedback to produce delicious meals that delighted both critics and diners alike. Chef Norman's ability to break through obstacles to communications and succeed in a hectic kitchens is an illustration of that universal language in food as well as the strength of passion and determination.

Vincent Tropepe

A renowned restaurateur and chef across the United States, Katsuya Fukushima was born with hearing impairment. Despite having communication issues within the kitchen Fukushima took his hearing impairment as an inspiration source and imagination, experimenting with new methods of cooking and flavors that have earned him acclaim worldwide. Because of his determination and persistence to his work, Chef Fukushima has shattering stereotypes and opened the door for chefs who are deaf to succeed in the world of gourmet food.

Well-known chef as well as author and TV celebrity, Yotam Ottolenghi was diagnosed with COVID-19. The condition temporarily hampered his sense of taste. Despite this Ottolenghi's continued efforts to create and invent at the kitchen, leveraging his vast knowledge of food and experience to create recipes that enthralled the senses and fed the soul. With his tenacity and imagination Chef Ottolenghi has influenced both home cooks and chefs to accept the challenges as opportunities for development and discovery in the field of culinary arts.

Chefs' stories of how they have overcome sensory challenges to master their culinary skills are powerful reminders of our human potential to be resilient, creative and flexibility. From Christine Ha's success in "MasterChef" and Chef Norman's mastery in French cuisine, these chefs have surpassed expectations and redefined the notion of what's achievable within the kitchen. Their experiences encourage us to take on new diverse challenges, appreciate diversity, and unleash their transformative powers to unite to, stimulate and nourish both the body and soul. As we consider their incredible accomplishments, let's honor their legacy by fostering inclusion access, innovation, and accessibility in the realm of culinary making

The Other Five Senses

sure that everyone has the chance for sharing the unique talents and talents to the world.

This will help you understand the reason why the five senses of humans aren't the only senses required to become a chef.

In the field of gastronomy the perception of smell, taste, touch, sight and hearing have long been thought to be the primary factor in the development of exceptional food experiences. But the core of true culinary mastery goes beyond the limits of the five senses, and encompasses the entire spectrum of sensory aspects that elevate cooking from food to an art. This work explores the multiple sensory aspects of culinary art, exploring the complex interplay between senses that go beyond the five senses of traditional and explaining the ways they contribute to skill of a chef.

The art of mastering the art of cooking is far more than the traditional five senses. It encompasses the entire spectrum of sensory aspects which elevate cooking to an experience that is transcendent. Chefs tap into a broad range of sensitivities and senses to create dishes that delight the senses, stir the mind, and feed the soul. In honor of the many facets sensory experience of culinary art Let us celebrate the unending imagination, passion and ingenuity that characterize the best chefs in the world that inspire us to appreciate every moment and revel in the pleasures of the culinary journey.

CHAPTER TWO

A Sense of Hospitality

Hospitality, in its concept and practice, covers an array of actions and values that create meaningful connections and improve the giver's and recipient's experiences. In this chapter, we will explore the fundamental aspects of hospitality and elaborate on its importance, cultural expressions, the importance of empathy, and its effect on both the professional and personal levels.

The art of hospitality brings together a range of human virtues, including kindness, generosity, respect, and a desire to make people feel appreciated and at ease. It transcends the fundamental host-hosting act and focuses on the basic human desire for belonging and connection. This chapter focuses on the core values that are the foundation of hospitality, its different forms, how it is portrayed in different contexts, and how it has remained an essential and beloved practice across various cultures and eras.

At the core of hospitality is the practice of generosity and kindness. It's about sharing one's resources—be it space or even time—with people, particularly those in need. Giving selflessly without the expectation of any reward distinguishes hospitality from transactions.

Hospitality is also rooted in respect for other people, recognizing and valuing each person's value. It is about actively listening and showing empathy while taking measures to ensure the comfort and well-being of others. Respect is universal and transcends ethnic, cultural, and social distinctions, and it is a crucial component in establishing trust and understanding.

Hospitality isn't a singular concept but a collection of different practices shaped by cultural, historical, and social influences. Every culture has unique taste in how hospitality is portrayed, perceived, and appreciated. This section explores the various cultural manifestations of hospitality and explains how these practices reflect broader social values and add to the diversity of world customs.

Beginning with an ancient Middle Eastern tradition of sharing meals, the Japanese notion of Omotenashi hospitality comes in different forms. Examining these diverse expressions gives insight into how societies consider hospitality and taking care of guests and the common threads that connect these traditions.

Food and drink play an essential role in hospitality in various cultures. Sharing meals is usually considered a universal symbol of openness and friendship that transcends language and cultural barriers. This article focuses on the significance of food as a part of hospitality rituals and how it functions as a means of communication and connection.

Empathy, the capacity to comprehend and understand the feelings of someone else, is at the heart of hospitality. It allows the host to anticipate and respond to guests' needs, creating a space of care and comfort. This article examines the impact of empathy on hospitality and its effect on the experience of both the host and the guest.

Genuine hospitality means being aware of and responding to the inexplicable demands of guests. It requires a thorough knowledge of human nature and an acute sense of observation. By anticipating the needs of their guests, hosts can create an inviting and comfortable environment that shows compassion and thoughtfulness.

The concept of hospitality extends beyond personal interaction and is an essential part of a variety of industries. In the workplace, hospitality impacts customers' satisfaction, loyalty, and a company's overall performance. This section explores the application of hospitality concepts in professional and personal situations, highlighting their importance in making lasting and positive impressions.

In the home, hospitality plays a significant part in building family relationships and bonds. It is about creating a welcoming environment for guests to feel welcome and as a part of the household.

In the business world, and especially in the hospitality industry, the idea takes on an organized form but still retains the core idea of giving guests a sense of care. This is how companies can integrate hospitality into their customer service, operations, and culture to enhance customer service and create brand loyalty.

Hospitality, which has its roots in human goodness and cultural expression, continues to be a powerful positive force in the world. It unites people, builds connections, and enhances our lives and communities. By embracing and practicing hospitality, we are open to new perspectives and experiences and the satisfaction of making others feel comfortable and appreciated. Whether through interactions with friends or professional pursuits, hospitality can change and lift, making it a lasting and universal value worth cultivating and preserving.

The Other Five Senses

In Ancient Greece, hospitality, also known as "Xenia," was a strict code of conduct for guests and hosts. It was administered by Zeus Xenios, the protector of travelers and responsible for the guest-host relationship. Xenia was a place where rituals were specific to hosting guests by providing food, shelter, and presents, and in return, guests were expected to be polite and not become a burden. This reciprocal bond demonstrated the mutual respect and trust between strangers, which reflected the Greeks' understanding of the bonds that all human beings have in common.

The tales of Greek mythology, epic poetry, and even the Bible, like The Odyssey of Homer "Odyssey," are replete with xenia, demonstrating its ideal practices and the devastating consequences of its infringement. The Odyssey, mainly, is an epic story that revolves around the notion of hospitality. Odysseus interacts with diverse kinds of xenia during his journey. These stories highlight the social importance of hospitality and its role in ensuring security, fostering alliances, and keeping God's favor.

In Ancient Rome, hospitality (hospitium) was a word with a somewhat different meaning; however, it was nevertheless significant. The formalization was higher, typically having a contractual connection between the host and the guest. Roman hosting wasn't only private but also a public obligation, which had consequences for social status and political alliances. The wealthy Romans would leave their residences (domus) for guests as a sign of their wealth and generosity, which helped to strengthen connections with the political system and increase their status within the social class.

It is believed that the Romans also had the God Jupiter Hospitalis, dedicated to protecting guests and overseeing the hospitality industry. This demonstrates the sacred aspect of hospitality within the Roman tradition, linking the divine and human realms through acts of kindness and respect toward guests.

As we move to the East, the concept of hospitality can take on a variety of styles, yet it remains a central cultural value. For example, in the past Persia, hospitality was considered a sign of God's moral obligation. The Avesta, a sacred Zoroastrian scripture, lauds its virtues in hospitality, insisting on the spiritual and moral advantages of showing hospitality and compassion for strangers.

In the ancient world of India, the notion in the ancient Indian concept of "Atithi Devo Bhava," which translates to "the guest's god," represents a deep respect for guests. This concept in the Hindu scriptures demonstrates the moral obligation to treat guests with the highest respect and kindness. It was not simply an act of social grace but rather an obligation of a higher order that offered spiritual rewards and strengthened the social web.

Similar to this, in the past China, Confucian ethics that emphasized: "ren" (benevolence) were extended to how guests were treated, emphasizing respect and considerate hospitality as an expression of moral excellence and virtue. Hospitality was also a means to show "li" (ritual respect for the law), which ensured that interactions between people were wholesome and reflected one's moral character.

The Silk Road was the trade route connecting two continents, East and West, and was an avenue for merchandise and exchanges between cultures. Along these routes, the caravanserais (roadside inns) served as food, shelter, and safety for travelers and traders and a symbol of hospitality in various cultures. These establishments were essential in the facilitation of trade. However, they also played an important part in facilitating the transfer of information, ideas, and customs about hospitality. The period is an excellent example of how hospitality transcended cultural and geographic borders, creating connections and mutual understanding between different peoples.

In the Middle Ages, Christian monasteries across Europe transformed into sanctuaries for travelers, pilgrims, and those in need and offered hospitality as a fundamental Christian obligation. This idea was built on Biblical doctrines and the example of Jesus Christ, emphasizing love and service toward strangers. Additionally, an edict of chivalry prevalent in the medieval period of Europe includes hospitality as one of the most important virtues. Knights and nobles were expected to provide shelter and security to those who were in need. This combination of religious obligation and the chivalric code established hospitality as a central moral and social tenet that shaped European ways of life and customs into the present.

From the historical perspective of hospitality, we can see its universal significance and lasting importance across eras and cultures. From ancient civilizations to medieval times, the concept of hospitality has been an expression of the values of humanity, a way to build connections and a method to ensure political and social cohesion. In the form of xenia and hospitium or the philosophical doctrines of Eastern traditions, hospitality has been evidence of the human capacity to show kindness, respect, and compassion. Knowing this rich tapestry of history is not just a glimpse into the past but also provides valuable tips for creating a more friendly and connected world in the present.

Hospitality, an idea as old as humankind itself, is reflected through a variety of practices and customs across the world, reflecting the diversity of human culture and philosophy. Its fundamental tenet, grounded in the morality of showing kindness to others, respect, generosity, transcends cultural and geographic borders and adapts to distinct forms and expressions in diverse societies.

In the Middle East, hospitality is not just a way of life but an essential part of life in the social sphere, infused with deep religious and cultural significance. Serving refreshments and food to guests, usually before any other contact, is a sign of deep gratitude and a friendly spirit. This custom is rooted in the desert culture, in which the harsh conditions have made hospitality an essential survival strategy. The sharing of resources, especially during times of shortage, was an ethical requirement as a gesture of kindness and reciprocity that has been practiced for long periods. This focus on hospitality is also evident in the scriptures of religion, which frequently stress the importance of extending hospitality to strangers and paying to meet their needs as a divine commandment.

In Japan, "Omotenashi" elevates hospitality to an art form, blending it with elegance, sensitivity, and deep anticipation. Omotenashi transcends mere service. It is about fully anticipating and meeting people's needs without expecting to receive anything in returned. This philosophy is apparent throughout Japanese culture, including the careful presentation of food and the meticulous arrangements of the guests' accommodations to ensure a peaceful experience. The Japanese tea ceremony, also known as "Chado," exemplifies Omotenashi in which every step and element is designed to show reverence and respect to the guest and create a sense of harmony and peace.

The Other Five Senses

Over the Atlantic in many Latin American cultures, hospitality is characterized by openness, warmth, and familial acceptance. People are generally treated as a part of the family, with little distinction between guests and their families. This kind of hospitality reflects an overall community ethos, which values close social bonds and a sense of well-being for all over individual security or privacy. Sharing meals, stories, or even houses with guests exemplifies the region's deep belief in community and solidarity.

In Africa, hospitality is also typical and a significant part of social life, with customs differing widely across its many cultures. Many African societies subscribe to the idea that guests bring joy to their homes and, as such, are treated with hospitality and respect. In certain societies, it is a norm that hosts provide the most luxurious accommodations and meals for their guests, even if the family has to settle for less. This is a way of expressing a culture of generosity and sharing and is understood as an occasion to be a part of a community and bond instead of an obligation or obligation.

The philosophical roots of hospitality, as explored by thinkers such as Emmanuel Levinas, provide a deeper, more universal meaning to these practices. Levinas believed that accepting people from the other is not merely a social convention but a fundamental ethical duty to our morality and identity in our lives as humans. This premise challenges us to think of hospitality not just as a set of rules but as a way of being in touch with the world and others in an open, compassionate, and respectful manner. It demands moral hospitality that acknowledges and respects everyone's dignity and values regardless of situation or background.

This kind of hospitality requires a willingness to be open to the other and to change by the experience. It is about listening with awe without judgment, letting go of judgment, and being genuinely interested in the stranger's story. This kind of hospitality could result in spaces of genuine dialogue and understanding, helping to bridge the gap between people and fostering a sense of human connection.

However, living a life of such hospitality comes with difficulties, particularly in a world characterized by increasing mobility and diversification, but also discrimination, conflict, and inequality. It requires the delicate balance of respecting one's own traditions while accepting the new in a world of generosity and respect for

Despite these difficulties, the universal significance of hospitality is a source of optimism and a reminder of the possibility of compassion and connections in human interactions. Whether through the elaborate rituals of Omotenashi, communal meals from Africa or Latin America, or desert hospitality in the Middle East, these practices have a common thread: the recognition of humanity as a whole and the power of treating people with respect and dignity.

As we navigate the complexity of modern life, the concept and practice of hospitality can teach us valuable lessons in ethics, empathy, and the practice of living in harmony. By embracing that spirit, we can build deeper bonds, appreciate our diverse cultures, and create an inclusive and compassionate world.

Hospitality is a continuum that extends beyond the intimate spaces of our homes to the vast and intricate network of the world's hospitality industry. Its practices, whether professional or personal, are based on the fundamental values of kindness, generosity, and the creation of warm and welcoming spaces. This allows us to explores the diverse nature of hospitality as it is embedded into everyday life and business operations.

The Other Five Senses

The heart of a person's hospitality is opening your home and life to the needs of others. It's an expression of hospitality and warmth that goes beyond mere social obligation. It becomes a sign of respect and care for those around you. This kind of hospitality could transform ordinary gatherings into memorable memories and build strong bonds of community and friendship. It is about being attentive to the requirements and needs of guests, making sure they feel welcome and appreciated. Whether it's a meticulously planned dinner party or a spontaneous offer of accommodation for someone in need, the core of hospitality is to make people feel welcome.

The concept of personal hospitality extends far beyond our home. It's evident in the little acts of kindness that we show strangers, the effort to make people feel welcome in our communities, and the help we give to those far from their homes. It's about creating environments - physical or emotional--where people feel comfortable and respected. They feel loved and valued. This kind of hospitality requires an intense feeling of compassion, a capacity to understand and listen to the feelings and needs of others, and an unwavering desire to help them feel better.

Moving from professional to personal The principles of hospitality are the same, but the size and scope shift dramatically. In the professional world, the hospitality industry now covers the entire globe and encompasses various services such as accommodation, food and beverages, travel, and tourism. It is not solely about individual acts of kindness but also about creating experiences that leave a lasting impression on guests. It's a complex mix of environments, services, and interactions, all of which aim to exceed and meet the expectations of customers and guests.

The art of hospitality is based on a thorough knowledge of customer requirements and preferences, a meticulous concentration on minor details, and the ability to identify and resolve issues. It's all about providing consistently high-quality, consistent service that makes customers feel valued and special. The idea is to create unforgettable moments that guests would like to revisit and be able to share with friends and family.

The challenges faced by professionals in hospitality are many and diverse. They include managing the logistical aspects of delivering service, maintaining the highest standards of quality, and coping with the unpredictable nature of customers' requirements and expectations. Professionals working in the hospitality industry require unique abilities, including excellent communication, leadership, and organizational skills, as well as the ability to think creatively and be flexible. They should also be proficient in directing resources, which includes time and financial and human capital, to ensure seamless guest experiences.

Furthermore, the hospitality industry is constantly changing due to changes in consumer behavior, technology, technological advancements, and global economic circumstances. This demands that professionals be adaptable and creative, constantly looking for methods to enhance their offerings and remain in the game. Sustainability is also a significant concern, as companies try to reduce their environmental footprint while providing excellent service. This ranges from cutting down on waste and conserving energy to finding ethical and local products.

At its heart, professional hospitality is about creating connections. This is about making your guests feel welcome and valued by creating a relationship beyond what is typically a transactional aspect of business. This requires a sense of hospitality embraced at every aspect of the organization, from the front-line personnel interacting directly with guests to the executive teams designing guidelines and policies. Creating a culture that is welcoming requires the training of employees and their empowerment by setting clear expectations and creating an atmosphere that is respectful and collaborative.

Professional hospitality's positive impact goes far beyond guests' simple experience. It is a critical factor in the world economy, creating jobs for a vast majority of people and making a significant contribution to the gross domestic product of numerous nations. The tourism and travel industry is an important economic growth driver, encouraging intercultural understanding and exchange. Tourism businesses also aid local communities by procuring locals for their products and services, as well as contributing to charities and taking part in community-based development initiatives.

The art of personal to professional hospitality reflects a universal set of principles and values that are the foundation of social interaction and human interactions. It's a factor that can alter personal experiences, improve communities, and spur economic growth. The warmth of an intimate meal with friends or the attentive attention to detail of a five-star accommodation is about creating moments of joy and connection that enhance our lives and connect people. As we traverse the challenges of modern life, the timeless values of hospitality have more relevance than ever before, informing us of the importance of generosity and kindness and the essential act of making someone feel at home.

Technology has transformed the hospitality industry, leading to unparalleled efficiency, customization, and enhancement of guest experiences. From the first point of contact to the feedback loop after a stay, the digital revolution has changed every aspect of the guest journey.

Online booking platforms have made it easier to access travel. They allow guests to search, reserve, and manage their accommodations with unimaginable ease. These platforms not only serve as a platform for booking reservations but also offer an abundance of information and reviews, allowing customers to make educated choices specific to their needs.

Virtual tours and Augmented reality (AR) applications give potential guests an insight into the facilities, accommodations, and locations before making the booking. This immersive technology can bridge the gap between expectations and reality, decreasing uncertainty and creating confidence between hosts and guests.

Artificial Intelligence (AI) and machine learning have brought personalization to new levels, allowing companies to provide personalized suggestions and services based on the study of large quantities of data. From personalized rooms and entertainment choices to customized dining experiences, AI aids in creating an unforgettable experience for every guest. Room features can be controlled by guests with smartphones or via voice commands, such as lighting, temperature, and entertainment systems, which improve comfort and ease.

However, despite all the technological advances, hospitality's essence has remained deep-rooted in human relationships. Technology is a tool to improve the quality of service. However, personal touch, such as a warm welcome or attentive service and genuine concern, are essential elements that technology can't duplicate. The biggest challenge and potential in the hospitality industry lies in using technology to enhance guests' experience while maintaining the human aspect, which is the essence of genuine hospitality.

The hospitality industry is looking toward the future, facing the challenge of taking on technological advances while maintaining the human element of hospitality. The future will be defined by a synthesis of tradition and modernity that will allow technology to enhance the quality of service without obscuring humanity.

Personalization will remain a significant trend as technology allows the development of more precise and predictive services. Artificial intelligence and big data will play vital roles in analyzing guest preferences and behavior, allowing for personalizing experiences on each level. However, the nature of hospitality will rely on using this data to improve human interactions rather than to replace them.

Ethics and sustainability also shape what the hospitality industry will look like shortly. As the awareness of environmental issues increases, guests seek experiences and accommodations that reflect their values. Technology can assist in this endeavor by providing solutions to reduce waste, energy consumption, and sustainable sources. However, the sector must ensure that technological advances are not at the cost of ethical business practices and the community's welfare.

The world's travel scene is becoming more interconnected as cultural exchanges become more common. Technology has made this possible, making it more accessible for people of diverse backgrounds to travel to new places and new cultures. The hospitality industry has to be aware of its guests' diversity, providing diverse and culturally sensitive experiences that reflect the diversity of its customers. In a world dominated by technological advances, the timeless spirit of hospitality has remained to humankind's experience. The concept of hospitality transcends transactional exchanges, expressing a culture based on kindness, generosity, and respect for others. It's about establishing mutually beneficial connections and creating memories that last for the rest of your life.

It is believed that the future of hospitality is not solely in technology but rather in the industry's ability to combine innovation with the fundamentals of human compassion and connections. By creating an environment that promotes both efficiency and compassion, the hospitality industry will remain successful, offering experiences that aren't just comfortable and personalized but also profoundly rewarding and fulfilling.

While the industry develops and evolves, we must remember that at the core of hospitality is the primary but fundamental action of making others feel valued, welcomed, and loved. This is the principle on which everything else is built. It's an affirmation that even in this world, which is constantly changing, the need for authentic connections is a constant. In embracing this idea, hospitality can overcome these challenges in the modern age and ensure that it will continue to be an agent for positive, significant connections in a connected world.

Chefs and cooks know that cooking is much more than a simple act. It's an expression of imagination as well as skill and passion! But do they have the ability to go beyond the simple task of preparing delicious food for guests? Exploring the diverse nature of hospitality in the culinary sector by exploring ways that chefs and cooks are involved in providing memorable dining experiences to their guests.

The Other Five Senses

In essence it is about creating an environment where people are able to feel welcome, comfortable and valued. It is a goal that is beyond the boundaries of the kitchen. Although cooking is an integral aspect of hospitality however, the role of a chef or cook involves more than making food, but also creating an atmosphere that is welcoming, engaging guests in discussions about their preferences and needs in order to deliver memorable dining experiences are important elements.

The chefs and cooks of hospitality are essential in ensuring a pleasant dining experience, ranging from food preparation to setting the mood and setting the mood for each event. From restaurant decor to preparation of the food, each element of dining affects its success and makes sure the dining experience is memorable for guests.

Executive chefs contribute to creating a welcoming dining environment as well as engaging their guests, and building connections through conversations and personal interactions. While diners may not be able to interact with their direct presence but their presence and experience are always apparent during a dining experience at any restaurant.

Certain chefs prefer to interact directly with guests via open kitchens that allow guests to observe the cooking process unfold or via dining experiences at the chef's table where guests eat in close proximity to the kitchen. This gives chefs the chance to showcase their culinary skills as well as answer questions regarding the dishes being served and provide insight into the dishes they serve. In more traditional dining establishments where chefs aren't able to be in direct contact with their guests however their impact will be felt in the food they prepare. Each dish is a reflection of their talent, creativity and personal taste and gives diners a glimpse into the chef's cooking concept and philosophy.

Chefs contribute to making dining an enjoyable experience by engaging with customers, catering for their guests' preferences and needs during their meal. This includes making food that is prepared according to the highest standards, but also catering to particular food preferences, restrictions or needs to ensure that every guest enjoys the dining experience.

Chefs collaborate with the front-of-house staff, like servers and sommeliers, to provide information on menus ingredients, preparation techniques, and unique tasting experiences for customers with food preferences or restrictions. They can also collaborate with their restaurant's chef team to create customized experiences for those with these preferences.

Chefs go the extra mile to satisfy guests' needs as well as preferences. Whether it involves modifying dishes to suit particular tastes or using local and seasonal ingredients to create memorable dining experiences. The personalized service can help create memorable dining experiences that will make guests return to return

Chefs are essential to hospitality through creating a welcoming environment and engaging guests, taking care of their preferences and needs during meals as well as catering for the complete guest's experience. Through understanding the many facets of hospitality, cooks and chefs can provide unique dining experiences and will leave lasting impressions on guests.

To fully comprehend what it is "to serve" others in hospitality it is necessary to dig deep into the concept. Serving is more than simple acts of help or offering; instead it is about anticipating and meeting people's needs that go beyond exchange. It is a result of compassion, empathy and a sincere desire to improve the well being and happiness of all people serving others is an ideal ethos that is evident in all aspects of hospitality.

In essence the concept of hospitality is to be of service by committing to creating a feeling of warmth, comfort and belonging to guests. It goes beyond the physical distribution of products or services but rather, it involves making meaningful connections, creating unforgettable experiences, and creating lasting impressions for those who receive it which is a true testament to the transformative power of human interaction and genuine concern and focus on particulars.

One of the most important aspects of hospitality is that of service anticipatory, that is being capable of recognizing the unspoken desires and needs of guests and respond to them prior to when they become apparent. For this to be done effectively, it requires the ability to observe and empathy as well as a deep understanding of human interaction. By anticipating the needs of guests before they are even triggered hospitality professionals show their commitment to providing individual and personal service that exceeds the expectations of guests.

Serving others in the hospitality industry means creating an ambience of warmth, hospitality and acceptance that makes guests to feel welcome and respected. This is not just about extraordinary technical knowledge and skills but as well genuine warmth and sincerity when interacting with guests. Hospitality professionals should display genuine interest and concern for the well being of guests, while establishing genuine relationships that go beyond mere transactions.

Vincent Tropepe

Professionals in hospitality are required to strive for excellence and continual improvement to ensure that guests have excellent experiences. This includes the quality of food and beverages, to cleanliness and ambience. Professionals in hospitality must constantly seek feedback, assess their the performance of their organization and pinpoint areas of improvement and growth by demonstrating a constant commitment to earn the trust of their patrons.

Another crucial aspect of delivering hospitality services efficiently is the ability to adapt and respond to changes in circumstances and guests' preferences swiftly and effectively. In order to do this successfully, you need adaptability, creativity and the ability to go beyond to meet guests' individual requirements and requests such as accommodating special diet restrictions, offering special accommodations or overcoming unexpected challenges hospitality professionals must be able to think quickly and come up with innovative enough to find solutions that surpass the expectations of guests.

Professionals in hospitality strive to create an environment of teamwork, collaboration, and mutual respect within their team members, which requires an effective way of communicating respect for differences, and a commitment to delivering the best customer experience. Working together in a harmonious manner and assisting one another within a supportive workplace that results in superior customer service.

A memorable dining experience is much more than simple nourishment; it's an immersive experience that stimulates all the senses, creates bonds and leaves an irresistible impression on the consumer. Every aspect of an exceptional dining experience can contribute to a customer satisfaction and overall wellbeing; we'll explore this impact in a multi-dimensional manner by studying the influence it exerts on customers their emotions, behavior, and perceptions.

A dining experience that is exceptional has one of the most profound effects on the emotional wellbeing of customers starting with being welcomed by friendly and warm staff, all the way to enjoying each bite, customers are immersed in a sense of joy, comfort and satisfaction The aromas and flavors are a feast for the senses. The ambience of the restaurant creates a sense of peace and relaxation.

A memorable dining experience can trigger all sorts of positive emotions in customers including excitement and happiness to nostalgia and comfort. Dining out can be an opportunity for customers to indulge in their senses and savor every moment they enjoy in the moment. A dining experience that is exceptional can create lasting memories for customers that which they'll treasure for a long time. Everything from exceptional service and amazing presentation of food, to the unforgettable atmosphere of restaurants can help create memories that people will treasure for the rest of their lives.

A memorable dining experience not just affects the consumer's emotions but also impacts their behavior and decision-making processes too. Studies have proven that customers are more likely to return to establishments where they've had positive dining experiences, highlighting the importance of providing outstanding service and high-quality to create customers' loyalty and a long-term relationship with the restaurant. A dining experience that is exceptional can have a hugely significant impact on consumers' purchasing decisions and the perception of brands.

Customers who have enjoyed their eating experiences tend to recommend a restaurant to friends and family members, and also praise it on social media and review websites which in turn influence attitudes and behaviors of others.

A dining experience that is exceptional enhances the perception of value that consumers have as they feel that they have received more value for the money they spent. Customers will spend more to experience dining that goes over and beyond expectations and offer outstanding service, quality or ambience providing a memorable experience makes it possible for restaurants to justify their higher prices and differentiate their offerings from those of competitors, while improving the perception of consumers about their value.

A dining experience that is exceptional creates an impression of exclusivity and a sense of prestige that enhances consumers' perceptions of worth. Customers will pay premium rates for dining experiences like dining experiences, tasting menus or chef's tables experiences and private dining events which offer memorable and unique experiences like tasting menus, chef's tables experiences, or private dining occasions. With these types of premium dining experiences in their restaurants, establishments can draw in discerning customers willing to spend more for high-end and services will be able to trust.

A great dining experience has profound effects on the consumer and their emotions as well as their behavior and perceptions in significant ways. From evoking positive feelings and creating lasting memories making purchase decisions more informed and

The Other Five Senses

influencing values - an outstanding dining experience will have an impact far beyond the restaurant. Through providing exceptional service and ambiance, restaurants can provide memorable experiences that keep people returning for more and bolster their standing as the best in their field.

The defining characteristic of the restaurant industry is the concept of excellence not only as a metric of achievement, but also as an essential element for expansion and constant improvement.

It is the foundation of outstanding guest experiences memorable experiences that enthrall and inspire, leaving lasting impressions on guests. They not only create the most powerful statement of our commitment to our customers as well as impact our team and their advancement in profound ways.

For restaurant teams, delivering extraordinary customer experiences is an area of immense satisfaction and pride. It proves their dedication as well as their dedication and attention to details; strengthening their commitment to being ambassadors for their restaurant's name and reputation. When customers offer praise or express their appreciation for exceptional service offered by staff members, it creates satisfaction while also raising morale and motivation within their staff.

Excellent guest experiences can create a profound impact on the team members of restaurants and their dynamics and culture. They encourage camaraderie, collaboration and support for each other when team members work together towards the same goal of meeting the expectations of guests and creating unforgettable dining experiences. This creates an atmosphere of empowerment in which everyone feels appreciated, valued and motivated to achieve their highest performance.

Restaurant teams can leverage excellent guest experiences to provide an opportunity to learn by demonstrating top practices, effective communications and problem-solving strategies in real time. When watching staff interact with guests, and then reflecting on their own interactions, employees get a better understanding of the underlying principles and methods to ensure excellent service. They are able to anticipate the needs of guests more efficiently while handling challenging situations with professionalism and poise and quickly adapting to ever-changing circumstances.

While aiding personal development and growth, outstanding guest experiences can also contribute to professional advancement for team members. These experiences help build a reputation within the industry, presenting individuals as competent and trustworthy individuals who are able to provide outstanding service in any situation which opens up opportunities for promotions, leadership roles, and training courses from owners of restaurants and managers who acknowledge exceptional performance as a part of their career development programs.

A great guest experience can serve as a reliable method of professional validation, confirming people's talents, abilities and contribution to the achievement of the restaurant. This kind of recognition not only boosts confidence and self-esteem but also creates an attitude of pride and ownership among employees who strive to be the best within their respective roles.

Experiential experiences that leave customers wanting more are a significant contributor to the sustainability and growth of a restaurant by fostering trust with customers, driving more repeat customers, and generating positive word-of-mouth recommendations. These interactions result in a positive cycle of prosperity and growth when satisfied customers become loyal customers who will spread the word of their experience to others, while bringing in new customers to come to your restaurant.

The experiences that are memorable for guests are not just testaments to the professionalism and dedication of staff members in restaurants but also a way to encourage professional and personal growth. Through consistently surpassing the expectations of guests with exceptional service, restaurant teams build an atmosphere that is a place of unity, excellence and continual improvement that set the stage for success in a competitive business. Through creating unforgettable dining experiences that please and inspire their guests Restaurant teams improve their own performance, while also advancing their careers, while ensuring the best future for themselves and for the restaurants they run.

Culinary art requires a distinct combination of creativity, skill and dedication to succeed but beyond technical proficiency and culinary knowledge are the other aspects that are crucial to become a renowned chef. Continuous development and hospitality are crucial in determining the career path.

At its heart hospitality is at the heart of culinary excellence and creates unforgettable dining experiences that last long in the memory of guests. Moving beyond the mere the act of cooking hospitality is a comprehensive approach to ensuring that guests are well-being as well as satisfaction and pleasure as a philosophy that renowned chefs acknowledge as each meal provides an opportunity to create lasting impressions, and to create lasting connections between diners.

The concept of hospitality in the context of food goes beyond the kitchen. It influences every aspect of dining experience from the ambience and presentation of food items to the manner in which staff members behave. A reputable chef is a symbol of this philosophy by creating an ambiance that is inviting, interacting with guests, and addressing their preferences and needs with a keen eye and attention to detail.

To be recognized as a leader in their field of culinary chefs need to possess not only outstanding technical abilities however, they must also possess genuine warmth, compassion, and hospitality. By focusing on the customer experience and exceeding guests' expectations in every way well-known chefs gain the respect and confidence of their patrons while also becoming the leaders in their field.

The top of the culinary revolution is the pursuit of excellence. This is something an experienced chef knows is essential in their quest. Continuous learning via the formal curriculum, practical experiences or co-working with others helps to keep up with the times while pushing new boundaries in the realm of creativity and innovation.

Continuous development spans an extensive array of tasks, ranging from experimenting with new techniques and ingredients to studying traditional culinary practices and the cultural influences. A skilled chef is constantly looking for inspiration and strives to broaden their menu of culinary choices in order to create dishes that are not just fantastic, but provide unforgettable experiences too.

Continuous improvement extends beyond the technical aspects to include other aspects of personal and professional development. Chefs who are respected know that mastery is a combination of humility, determination and a flexible spirit that is able to take on changes and change to it.

Being relevant in today's constantly changing world of food requires constant development and willingness to embrace innovation and changes. The most successful chefs are regarded for their pioneering spirit, who break conventions and push the boundaries of culinary creativity more then ever. They do this by focusing on the pursuit of continuous learning and creating an environment that encourages the pursuit of innovation and experimentation These chefs are a source of inspiration for others, while leaving an imprint in the history of food and drink.

Hospitality and a dedication to continual development are the key elements of being a renowned chef. Hospitality is the basis on which excellence in culinary can thrive as continuous development will result in continual development and innovation. Together, these elements form the foundation of every chef's success, and shape the way they cook as well as service delivery and their professional development. Chefs who are respected recognize that their hospitality goes beyond just a concept; it's an attitude that guides their work in all aspects. In putting emphasis on hospitality, well-known chefs make dining experiences that don't just taste great but also are memorable and profoundly significant as well.

Continuous improvement is essential to stay in the forefront of culinary fields and staying relevant in an the ever-changing world of food. Professional chefs are aware of this by expanding their comfort zones the limits of their expertise, exploring new ideas and embracing the challenges head on. Through a focus on continuous development and advancement, they stay at the forefront of culinary creativity, while encouraging others to follow their lead. A commitment to hospitality and continuous growth are crucial to becoming a renowned chef. In focusing on guest experience and embracing opportunities for lifelong learning and pushing culinary innovation limits, chefs will achieve the status of industry leaders while leaving an indelible impression on the culinary world across the globe.

CHAPTER THREE

A Sense of Self and Culinary Identity

Culinary identity is a multifaceted and complex concept that goes beyond eating as a mere activity. It's a vast tapestry woven from the various threads of our experiences, culture, and preferences. The uniqueness of this identity isn't solely about what we eat; it's about what we eat and the significance and meanings that we place on food. It's a way to express ourselves and what we're about, our origins, and what we believe in. In this chapter, we'll look into the subtleties of identity in food and touch lightly on the role played by the senses in defining our food-related environment.

The culinary identity is inextricably linked with our self-image. It expresses our journey, history, and interactions with the world surrounding us. Food is more than food; it's a way by which we can connect, celebrate our culture, and look for new possibilities. The tastes we enjoy, the food we adore, and the traditions we cherish all contribute to the broader picture of our culture.

The core of a culinary identity is the powerful influence of cultural heritage. The food we grew up with as children, the recipes passed through generations, and the traditions we follow in the kitchen are all rich in the significance of culture. These customs give us the feeling of belonging and continuity that connects us to our past and cultural roots. They testify to our forefathers' resiliency, creativity, and adaptability, who created dishes that fed their bodies and enhanced their culture.

Personal experiences play an essential role in shaping our culinary identity. The sensory experiences associated with food - the smell of a simmering stew, the sour taste of a fresh fruit, or the sound of a hot oil simmering are permanently etched into our minds, triggering memories and emotions that are our own. These experiences are the basis of our tastes and preferences for food, which influence how we view and appreciate food.

Individual preferences add a layer of complexities to our culinary identity. Our tastes, preferences, food choices, diet, and philosophy reflect our personalities, lifestyles, and values. Many elements shape them, such as health issues, ethics, moral beliefs, and environmental issues. As we move through our lives the way we live, our values may change and reflect changes in our surroundings, knowledge, and outlook.

The interaction of these components creates a vibrant and ever-changing identity for food. It's a living thing constantly adjusting to new experiences, influences, and insights. Our culinary identity grows and changes as we experience various cultures, explore new ingredients and interact with diverse cuisines. It is a dazzling tapestry of our development, interaction with our world, and daily journey.

The importance of our senses in determining our food identity is not to be underestimated. Taste, smell, and hearing are all interconnected to our culinary experiences. They are the means through which we can perceive and appreciate the subtleties of texture, flavor, and smell. The senses play a significant part in shaping our memories of food and preferences, impacting our choices and forming our food preferences and identity.

The Other Five Senses

The sense of taste is possibly the most tangible and significant sense of these. It is the primary method by which we perceive and judge food. The flavors we taste- sweet, sour, bitter, salty, and umami - are crucial to our food preferences and sense of self. They are the basis of our tastes, which are deeply personal and memorable. The scent is closely connected to taste, amplifying and enhancing food flavor. The smell of food will transport us to various locations and moments, creating memories and feelings. It plays an essential part in our anticipation and satisfaction with food and adds depth and dimension to our dining experience.

Also, sight plays a significant part in shaping our identity. How food is presented visually affects how we perceive its taste and quality. Food's shapes, colors, and textures all form part of what makes it appealing and contribute to our dining experience. Hearing and touch may seem less apparent in their effects. However, they're equally important. Food texture, felt through touch, impacts our satisfaction and enjoyment. The sounds of food, such as the crunch of an apple and the smack of bacon frying, are a further layer of sensory pleasure.

Culinary identity is a vibrant and intricate concept that covers numerous aspects. It reflects our cultural background, personal experiences, and preferences, which are formed by the complicated interaction of our senses. While we live our lives, our food preferences continue to evolve as we live, reflecting our development and interaction with those surrounding us. It's a testimony to the variety and depth of human life, a celebration of our distinctive preferences, and a homage to the universal culinary language.

Vincent Tropepe

At the core of our culinary identity lies the past. Foods we consider typical or a symbol of our culture are often linked to the past. These meals tell stories of celebration, survival, and a sense of community. They result from many years of innovation and adaptation influenced by the environment and socio-economic and historical occasions. For instance, the usage of corn in Mexican food can be traced to the early civilizations of Mesoamerica. The use of rice in Chinese dishes reflects this region's agricultural methods.

Culture plays an integral part in shaping our food culture. It defined the readily available ingredients and appreciated the most popular cooking techniques, as well as the occasions that are characterized by certain food items. For instance, the Mediterranean diet, rich in olive oil, fruit, and seafood, expresses the area's bounty. In the same way, the elaborate tea rituals of Japan are a symbol of culture that has influenced the country's food culture.

On a personal scale, our journey significantly impacts our taste. The foods we are raised eating, the foods we identify with nostalgia and comfort, and the food traditions we adopt add to our distinctive gastronomic identity. The culinary identity is very personal and can differ from person to person. Familiar customs, personal preferences, and life experiences determine the influence. It could be the spiciness of a family recipe handed through generations, whereas, for others, it could be the blend of tastes discovered during traveling and exploration.

Culinary identity isn't unchanging; it is susceptible to change and development. Our culinary preferences and methods change as we experience new cuisines, cultures, and cooking methods. This flexibility is an essential aspect of the food identity. It signifies our ability to incorporate new tastes into our current structure, resulting in a dynamic and ever-changing food landscape. For instance, the rise of fusion food shows how different culinary styles can mix and change, leading to innovative dishes that transcend traditional cuisine's boundaries.

Ingredients and methods are the basis of a culinary identity. The availability of specific ingredients is often a sign of regional cuisines, whereas cooking techniques are often a hallmark of the culinary traditions of a particular culture. Spices used to spice Indian food preparation, for instance, are not only an issue of taste but also a reflection of traditional trade routes and preferences. The smoking method in American barbecue is rooted in the conventional cooking methods of the Indians and has developed into a distinctive feature of American cuisine.

In our globalized age, the culinary experience is more complicated than ever. The convenience of traveling and the accessibility of a broad range of ingredients have led to an intermixing of culinary traditions. This has led to distinct culinary styles and a mix of different influences. For example, Tex-Mex cuisine blends with Mexican and American food traditions, and the rising popularity of sushi within Western countries has prompted variations such as the California roll.

Culture plays an integral part in developing our identity. The ingredients, flavors, and cooking techniques of a particular region express the region's history, geography, and social structure.

The link between food and culture is a fundamental part of the social fabric. Food isn't only a way to eat but also a symbol of culture, a symbol of community identity, and a vehicle for telling stories. Through food, cultures keep their traditions alive, celebrate their festivals, and convey their beliefs. Traditions of food are passed down through generations, with each dish containing the wisdom and stories passed down through time.

The region's history is a significant factor in creating its distinctive culinary style. Historical events like conflict, migrations, and trade have affected the availability of ingredients and the evolution of cooking methods. For instance, the Columbian Exchange, the widespread transfer of animals, plants, and people across and between the Americas and the Old World, drastically changed the cuisines across both countries. It brought tomatoes to Italy, potatoes to Ireland, and chili peppers to India. It led to the development of iconic recipes like spaghetti with tomato sauce, Irish stews, and hot Indian curries.

Geography plays an essential aspect in determining a particular region's food identity. The climate, terrain, and natural resources within a specific area determine the varieties of food vegetables that can be produced and the types of animals that can be bred, affecting the ingredients used in cooking. For instance, coastal regions typically have a long tradition of seafood-based dishes, whereas areas with mountains could prefer preserved foods like pickled and dried meats and vegetables.

The social structure of a society is another significant factor in developing its culinary identity. Values and norms of society influence the way food is prepared in a variety of ways, from the kinds of foods that are accepted to eat to the way food is cooked and consumed. Food is a significant element of social gatherings and rituals in certain societies, but it is more practical in others. The importance of food in the social context can reflect larger social structures, like gender, class, and power dynamics.

Furthermore, the culinary identity isn't just about the traditional dishes of an area but also how these dishes are altered and reinterpreted as time passes. When people move, and cultures meet, the culinary traditions blend and develop, giving birth to new fusion foods. This mixing of culinary traditions indicates the vitality of culture and the constant interchange between ideas and influences.

In our modern, globalized world, the food culture of regions is also influenced by external factors, ranging from the importation of ingredients to the rising popularity of international culinary styles. However, even as global trends affect local foodscapes, there is a growing interest in preserving and celebrating traditional cooking practices to protect the cultural legacy and encourage sustainable development.

The role played by the culture of a region in shaping its culinary identity is multifaceted and complex. The ingredients, flavors, and cooking techniques of a particular area are not only reflections of its geography, history as well as social fabric but are also an expression of its heritage and its identity. When we discover the many food traditions around the globe, we understand our intricate cultural tangles.

Our experiences as individuals are a significant factor in developing our food preferences. From the food we grew up in childhood to the foods associated with home and comfort, every meal can create our unique food-related footprint. These experiences aren't just about food and the accompanying feelings, memories, and connections.

The power of food to trigger memories is awe-inspiring. The scent of freshly baked bread could instantly bring us back to our mother's kitchen. Amazingly, we watched as she kneaded and formed the dough using skilled hands. The taste of a classic dish may remind us of family gatherings where laughter and stories were shared over large plates. These experiences of sensory experiences are permanently imprinted into our minds as the basis for our identity as foodie.

Our palates, tastes, and culinary preferences grow and expand as we age. Foods we used to turn to might become comfort food, and the ingredients you didn't even know existed to be the staples of our kitchens. Every new experience adds a dimension to our food culture and enriches it with richness and depth.

Those whose food choices have influenced us determine our taste in food. Friends, parents, grandparents, and chefs we haven't met make an impression on our food preferences. Recipes handed through generations are a source of the stories and traditions of our past, linking us to our culture and ancestors. People who help us discover new dishes and cuisines can broaden our culinary options, bringing diversification to our diets and our identity.

The places we've lived in and have traveled to contribute to creating our own culinary identity. A life in a beach area can instill a love for seafood, and a stay in bustling cities could inspire a love of street food. Traveling can expose us to an array of tastes and cooking styles that allow us to integrate elements from diverse cuisines into our cooking, broadening our culinary horizons. As we move through our lives, our food-related identity changes. It expresses our journey, experiences, and the people and locations that have influenced our lives. It's a means to hold the memories of our lives, celebrate our culture, and bond with other people. Our culinary identity reflects who we are in the food language.

The Other Five Senses

The evolution of culinary identity is a fluid process shaped and formed by myriad elements that interact in intricate ways. While we travel through our lives and encounter new ingredients, flavors, and different cultures, we constantly alter our food landscape, adding an extra dimension and depth to our food choices.

Travel plays a vital role in this process. Suppose we travel outside of the familiar and open ourselves to new tastes. Every place has its distinctive culinary traditions, recipes, and cooking techniques. For instance, an excursion to Thailand could bring us closer to the fresh flavors of galangal and lemongrass, and a trip to Mexico might open our eyes to the rich, smoky flavor of chipotle peppers. These experiences don't just broaden our culinary options but can also affect our cooking style and taste preferences as we return home.

The merging of diverse cuisines is another reason to change our identity as a foodie. People of different backgrounds mix and share their cultural heritage, which leads to the development of new dishes that combine the flavors and techniques of various culinary styles. The result is a fusion that can take place in many different settings, from multicultural homes to urban cosmopolitan areas where global culinary styles are readily available. It results in a food landscape that is continuously changing to reflect the constantly changing landscape of our increasingly global world.

The change in food culture is also influenced by personal growth and experiences. As we get older and become more accustomed to our diets, our tastes and requirements may change, causing us to experiment with different cooking techniques and ingredients. For instance, health concerns can make us try vegan recipes or grain alternatives. Also, significant life occasions, like starting an extended household or moving to a brand new country, could influence our choices in food and drink.

Environmental and social factors influence our perception of food as time passes. The increasing awareness of sustainable and eco-friendly eating has prompted many to choose locally-sourced organic, sustainable ingredients. This trend isn't just impacting our individual choices for food but also influences more significant changes in the food industry, including the farm-to-table movement and the rise of vegan and vegetarian cuisines.

Technological advancements have also changed our cooking and eating habits. Social media and websites have helped make it simpler to find recipes, cooking methods, and culinary inspiration from all over the globe. The democratization of knowledge in the kitchen allows home cooks to explore different flavors and cuisines and further enhance their culinary identities.

In addition, the evolution of a persons culinary identity will be affected by the interaction between tradition and modernity. While we can appreciate the recipes handed over to generations, we also try to add our twist to them and adapt them to our personal preferences and style. The balance between respecting the past and taking a step forward is essential to our food's evolution.

The development of a persona in the culinary world is a continuous process formed by various elements, including travel and the fusion of cultures, personal experiences, technological advances, social trends, and the delicate balance between traditions and new ideas. While we traverse this path, our food identity constantly reflects what we're about, where we've been, and where we're going in a world of ever-expanding flavors and experiences.

The Other Five Senses

Self-expression and identity are entwined. When we enter the kitchen, we're not only cooking; we are performing an act of personal story telling. Every ingredient we use, technique we choose, and every food we cook expresses our life, experiences, and uniqueness. The food we cook is an opportunity to draw our own stories. A carefully crafted gourmet meal could express our commitment to excellence and precision, showing our talents and appreciation for the finest items in our lives. However, an accessible, comforting food item could be a powerful testimony to our desire for simplicity and warmth, our connection to our roots, and our desire to offer food and comfort to our family members.

Our food preferences are often determined by our culture, which carries the flavors of our ancestors and the culture of our time. A recipe passed down over generations isn't simply a list of directions. It's a connection with our history, a method to honor those who came before us and to preserve their memories and keep them alive. When we prepare these traditional meals and recipes, we're not only conserving a recipe. We maintain a part of our culture, a link to our roots that has stood the ages.

The tastes we enjoy reflect our character. A person who likes hot, spicy food may be considered brave and bold, whereas an affinity for delicate, soft flavors may signify a fan of balance and refinement. The choices we make in the kitchen are reflections of our personalities and a reflection of our personality.

Furthermore, the way we serve our food is also an act of self-expression. A beautiful plate is an artwork expressing creativity and a chance to participate in the experience of a sense. It's a way to communicate our aesthetic sensibilities and care for detail, making a meal an event. In the current globalized environment, food identity expresses our willingness to explore new experiences and our openness to the diverse nature of life. Innovating with different flavors from various cuisines, including exotic ingredients in our food and fusing traditional culinary practices, broadens our perspectives and shows an international outlook.

In addition, our choices in food are a reflection of our beliefs and values. Choosing local, organic ingredients expresses our belief in sustainability and environmental accountability. Adopting a vegan or vegetarian lifestyle could reflect our ethical beliefs and allow us to align our eating habits with our beliefs. In times that are a celebration, food can be an opportunity to share joy and to express gratitude. The celebration of food is a means to bring families together, celebrate important occasions, and make new memories. Through our food, we express our joy and determination to spread it around by turning a meal into an event to celebrate life.

However, food can provide comfort and an avenue for showing sympathy during grief. Making a meal from scratch for grieving people is an act of compassion and kindness and offers comfort and encouragement by using a universal food language. The culinary identity is also an evolving entity that changes as we experience life and the changing environment.

Cooking is often a process of personal growth and self-discovery. When we master new techniques, try new recipes, and improve our abilities, we learn our abilities and personal preferences. The kitchen is a place for experimentation and exploration, allowing us to test our limits and unleash our imagination. Identity and self-expression in the kitchen are inextricably linked. Through the food we make and how we serve it, we convey our identity, who we are, where we are from, and our beliefs. Our choices in the kitchen are an expression of our character and our cultural heritage as well as our beliefs, and they are a satisfying and balanced method of expressing our identity.

Accepting and understanding ourselves is vital to personal growth that profoundly influences our work lives. It is important to be aware of ourselves and acknowledge our characteristics and how these aspects affect our choices in career as well as workplace relationships, the way we lead, and our overall success in our professional lives.

Awareness of our unique characteristics is crucial to personal development that can profoundly impact your professional life. This process requires acknowledging and accepting our individuality, including the characteristics and traits that define us. Acceptance isn't always straightforward, particularly in a culture that prefers uniformity and conformity. It is, however, an essential step toward realizing our true selves and finding success in our professions.

One of the primary aspects of accepting our characteristics is acknowledging that our flaws are a part of our human nature. Instead of chasing the unattainable goal of perfect perfection, we can recognize the beauty of our imperfections and the lessons they can teach us. This change in perspective helps us look at our work and personal lives with acceptance and humility, which are essential in any professional environment.

The quality of authenticity, which comes from acceptance, is a trait that is highly appreciated at work. When we are authentic, we bring all of our self to work, bringing our unique views, thoughts, and approaches to solving issues. This could lead to more innovative and creative solutions and satisfaction and enjoyment from our working experience. Being authentic can also help build more authentic, trusting connections with our colleagues and clients, which are essential to lasting success in the workplace. In addition, acknowledging our individuality can increase confidence in ourselves and boost our self-esteem. When comfortable with our uniqueness and who we are, we're more likely to defend our beliefs and values regardless of the opposition. This self-confidence can allow us to face new opportunities and challenges, leading to personal development and career progress.

Acceptance does not mean we must settle down or stop pursuing improvement. It is crucial to realize that while we must be proud of our unique qualities, we can also work to develop new abilities and enhance our strengths. The trick is to do this from the perspective of self-love and acceptance instead of self-criticism and feeling inadequate. Apart from the advantages of being ourselves, accepting our individuality can positively impact the workplace. Comfortable people being themselves create a more diverse and inclusive workplace. This variety of thinking and experiences can result in better, more effective solutions and an enlightened and harmonious work environment.

Acceptance can reduce anxiety and stress, which are typical n high-pressure workplaces. If we're constantly trying to conform to a mold or achieve unrealistic expectations, this can be detrimental to our emotional and mental well-being. When we accept our limitations and self-acceptance, we can approach work with a sense of calm and self-confidence, resulting in better productivity and job satisfaction.

It is important to remember that acceptance is a continuous and never-ending process. Our personalities and circumstances could alter over time, and what we consider acceptable about ourselves now could change soon. The ongoing process of self-discovery, acceptance, and discovery can be challenging but rewarding because it allows us to continue changing and growing as professionals and individuals. Accepting the uniqueness of our personality is an essential aspect of personal growth that can significantly influence how we conduct our lives professionally. It lets us embrace our individuality, promote authenticity, and boost confidence, vital to successful careers. Recognizing and appreciating the strengths that distinguish us can lead to an enjoyable and fulfilling professional experience.

A thorough awareness of our strengths and abilities helps us choose jobs that align with our core values. If our work matches our persona and values, we are more likely to experience satisfaction. This is essential since it guarantees that we're not doing work for a paycheck and are involved in pursuits that bring us joy and a sense of achievement. It's the difference between getting up every morning with a fear of the day ahead and getting up to tackle new opportunities and challenges. Suppose we pick a job that reflects our personality. In that case, we will be more likely to succeed because our unique abilities and passions drive us to push ourselves above and beyond.

Being and knowing our self-worth allows us to communicate with coworkers in a way that is authentic and confident. It encourages genuine connections and cooperation vital to a desirable work environment. If we feel comfortable in our skin, speaking up, communicating our thoughts, listening to others, and developing lasting relationships are more accessible. These relationships are at the heart of a positive and productive workplace where everyone feels appreciated and a part of the team. Genuine interactions also result in excellent communication, as employees are more likely to share their feelings and thoughts openly, leading to more efficient problem-solving and creativity.

Self-aware leaders genuinely inspire respect and trust. They foster a positive atmosphere that makes team members feel appreciated and inspired. Authentic leaders demonstrate their leadership by showing vulnerability and self-confidence and encouraging others to emulate them. They also excel in recognizing and exploiting each member's strengths because they realize that a wide range of perspectives and skills will result in better results. These leaders aren't unwilling to admit that they aren't able to provide every answer, which helps create an environment of growth and learning. Their honesty builds a solid base of trust, which is vital for a productive team or business.

Knowing our strengths and weaknesses helps us adjust to changes and challenges in the professional world. This lets us leverage our strengths and find support when we're less confident. In today's dynamic and constantly changing working environment, flexibility is essential. If we're aware of our strengths, it is easy to recognize the situations that play to our strengths and recognize when we'll need to build new abilities or seek help. Self-awareness helps us be aware of our growth and learning, ensuring that we are relevant and effective in our roles.

Understanding our personal needs and limits is essential to maintain an appropriate balance between work and life. It helps prevent burnout and ensures we can make time for personal development and relationships. If we know what we require to feel content inside and outside of work, we can create boundaries that allow us to take on work demands while caring for our well-being. This is crucial for long-term success because it helps prevent burnout and keeps us focused and focused in our jobs.

The impact of self-awareness and acceptance of ourselves in your professional life is significant. It impacts our career choices and relationships at work, determines our leadership style, improves our flexibility, and assists us in maintaining an appropriate balance between work and life. Accepting ourselves and understanding ourselves allows us to navigate our professional lives with confidence, honesty, and a sense of purpose, leading to a more satisfying and productive career.

Self-examination is a crucial step to personal growth. It requires contemplation, reflection, and the willingness to examine our inner world. This process is vital to cultivating self-awareness, encouraging personal development, and moving through life with more focus and clarity.

Self-examination involves a reflective process designed to increase our knowledge of who we are. It examines our values, beliefs, motives, actions, and motivations to discover the core of who we are and the underlying reasons for our actions. This requires honesty, sincerity, and the willingness to confront complex facts.

The Steps of Self-Examination

- **Setting Goals:** Begin with clear intentions to begin your self-examination journey. Decide what you want to accomplish, whether finding clarity on a particular problem, understanding your triggers for emotional reactions, or identifying areas of personal development.

- **Creating a Reflective Space:** Dedicate a quiet, comfortable space for reflection. This could be a tangible space, such as a cozy corner of your house or a peaceful space that allows you to concentrate on your thoughts without distractions.
- **Journaling:** Writing is an effective tool to examine yourself. Write about your thoughts, feelings, emotions, experiences, and patterns. Don't be a slave to your thoughts. Allow them free flow.
- **Questioning Probing Questions:** Consider challenging yourself by asking deep and probing questions. Ask yourself questions about your core values, biggest fears, favorite achievements, and areas where you are unhappy or stuck.
- **Asking for Feedback**: Self-perception could be biased. Ask for feedback from trusted friends, family members, or therapy to gain an outside perspective of your behavior and patterns.
- **Practice Mindfulness:** Mindfulness-based techniques like meditation or deep breathing will help you remain focused and present during self-examination. They also allow you to recognize your thoughts and feelings without judging.
- **Finding Patterns:** Seek out common themes within your journal's comments, feedback, and reflections. These patterns can give you valuable insights into your behavior and your beliefs.
- **Facing discomfort:** Self-examination frequently leads to uncomfortable emotions. Instead of avoiding them, we should accept them as one of them. They're a signpost to areas of expansion.

The Other Five Senses

Based on your understanding, establish specific, attainable goals to help you grow personally. The goals you set should align with your goals and values. Re-examination and revision is a continual process. Review your reflections regularly and goals to evaluate your progress, and make adjustments when necessary.

Your resistance could be internal resistance to confronting unsettling facts about your self. It's normal to feel this way. However, it's crucial to work through it to develop a deeper awareness of yourself. Reflection is essential, and excessive thinking can cause analysis insanity. It would help to strike the right balance between mindful contemplation and decisive actions.

Self-examination may cause intense emotions. It is essential to have strategies for dealing with stress, such as conversing with a friend or trying relaxation methods.

We all have biases that may affect our perception of ourselves. Be aware of these biases and seek to achieve objectivity with your thoughts. The risk is being too reflective and unable to translate your insights into the right actions. Be sure that your self-analysis results in tangible changes to your life.

Self-examination increases self-awareness by helping you recognize your weaknesses, strengths, and core values.

With more awareness of yourself, you can make choices that align with your authentic self and long-term objectives. Knowing yourself better allows you to communicate and establish stronger relationships. A self-analysis serves as an effective way to improve your personal development that allows you to recognize and address areas of improvement. By identifying how your triggers affect you emotionally and the patterns, you can devise strategies for coping to increase your resilience in the face of difficulties.

Self-examination is an arduous process that requires honesty, courage, and dedication. It's an essential tool to develop our personal lives and provides insights that allow individuals to live their lives more fully and effectively. When we embrace this process of introspection, it will enable us to navigate the complexities of life with greater awareness and strength, resulting in a more meaningful and satisfying life.

Self-examination is one of the most essential steps for personal and professional development and self-improvement. It's the act of taking a look at our thoughts, emotions, and behavior to gain a greater understanding of ourselves. Introspection is a must for several reasons.

One of the most essential advantages of self-reflection is its ability to determine strengths and weaknesses. Through reflection on our previous events, actions, and choices, we can identify areas in which we excel and areas where we could improve. This knowledge is vital to personal growth since it helps us leverage our strengths while addressing the places where we are weak.

Self-examination helps us to understand our triggers for emotional reactions. This includes specific instances or situations that trigger intense emotional responses. We can devise strategies to control our emotions when we recognize these triggers. This is crucial in stressful situations where the ability to control our emotions can dramatically influence our choices and interactions with other people.

A third and crucial aspect of self-reflection is identifying behavior patterns. We often do certain things without thinking about it, even though they're not helping us. We can discern these patterns and identify their root reasons by examining ourselves. This information helps us overcome negative patterns and to adopt more constructive behavior.

Self-examination is the first step to making positive changes to our lives. By having a clear awareness of our strengths and weaknesses, emotional triggers, and behavior patterns, We can establish achievable goals and create concrete plans to reach these goals. This method of personal development leads to a happier and more enjoyable life.

Self-examination also plays a vital role in building more healthy relationships. By recognizing our preferences, limits, boundaries, and communication style and boundaries, we can communicate with others more effectively. Self-awareness allows us to speak clearly, constructively solve conflicts, and create more robust, lasting connections.

The information gained through self-reflection will help us make better personal and professional decisions. If we know our priorities, values, and biases, we can make decisions more aligned with our authentic selves. This leads to improved outcomes in both our professional and personal lives.

Self-examination promotes self-acceptance and helps us accept every aspect of ourselves, including our imperfections and limitations. Being fully accepting of ourselves is essential to self-love, and self-compassion. These are vital to overall wellbeing and happiness.

Self-examination is a practice that promotes mindfulness, which is a state of being aware and fully present in the present. Practicing mindfulness improves our self-awareness, allowing us to respond to life's challenges more calmly and clearly.

Self-examination promotes personal responsibility. Acknowledging our role and taking responsibility for our actions helps us make positive changes. This sense of accountability is crucial to personal growth and achievement.

Self-examination, in the end, is a path to self-discovery. It lets us discover our innermost parts, uncover our hidden sides, and reconnect with our most cherished dreams and desires. Self-discovery is a continuous process that can enrich our lives in many ways. Ultimately, the significance of self-examination to develop your character can't be overemphasized. It's a powerful instrument that allows us to know ourselves better, make better decisions, and live more fully. Through this practice, we can unlock our true potential and live a more satisfying life.

The culinary identity of a person is an expression of our personal journey, culture, and preferences. A distinct combination of tastes, experiences, and practices defines our relationship with food. This study explores three essential aspects of a culinary identity: mastering the craft of becoming a pastry chef, the allure of a particular cuisine, and the ambiance of different dining experiences.

The profession of a pastry chef is an artistic art that goes far beyond the simple preparation of sweets. It's a form of self-expression where each pastry chef can bring their vision, imagination, and passion to the making. The profession of pastry chef isn't solely about following recipes. It's about incorporating personal flair and creativity into each creation. Pastry chefs are similar to sculptors, using sugar, flour, and butter for their material. They mold these simple ingredients into masterpieces that entice the palate and please the eyes. The precision required for pastry production is comparable to that needed by scientists because even the slightest deviation in the measurements could cause a drastically different result. Attention to the smallest of details is what differentiates most exceptional pastry chefs.

The persona of pastry chefs is dependent on their selection of ingredients. The quality of the ingredients is crucial since the highest quality ingredients produce the most satisfying outcomes. It doesn't matter if it's finding the best vanilla bean made from only the finest chocolate or selecting the most fresh fruits; every ingredient contributes to creating the finished product. This dedication to quality expresses the chef's passion for their art.

Techniques are an additional aspect of the identity of a pastry chef. From the technique of tempering the chocolate to the precise art of creating perfect layers of pastries, The techniques are perfected over time through training and experiments. The ability to master these skills is an indication of the patience and perseverance of the chef. The presentation is the final element that brings a pastry chef's masterpiece to life. It's the culmination point of their ideas and harmonizes every component. No matter what it is, just a simple dusting of sugar powdered or an elaborate edible design, The presentation makes every dessert visually appealing.

The path of a pastry chef goes through continuous change. Food is constantly changing, and new techniques and trends appear daily. A good pastry chef is flexible and eager to study and try new things.

The willingness to experiment and learn makes their work new and exciting, ensuring they are at the culinary world's top. The search for perfection is the primary motivation in the work of a pastry chef. They are on a mission to create the perfect dessert that tastes delicious and inspires emotion. It's about pushing the boundaries of what's possible and constantly striving to take the enjoyment of dessert to new levels.

Being a pastry chef is an experience that requires imagination and precision, as well as the constant search for excellence. It's a job that requires a passion for the culinary arts and the desire to continue development and improvement. If you're willing to take on the journey, the rewards are sweet, and they can share their delicious creations with the world and bring happiness and joy to those who enjoy their dishes.

Cuisine, a rich and intricate mix of aromas, flavors, and cultures, gives a window into a society's essence. It's more than just an assortment of food items, but a fabric woven with the threads of geography, history, and the spirit of its inhabitants. The intense, hearty flavors of Italian food, the intricate and fragrant spice of Indian dishes, and the simple beauty of Japanese food are all testimony to the many stories diverse cuisines have to be able to tell.

The pull of a particular type of food on our identity as a culinary professional is unquestionable. It could be due to our ancestors' food, which connects to our roots and heritage. Or, it could be a dish we came across and loved while traveling, which swept us away on a delicious travel experience and left an unforgettable impression on our palates. It could be in tune with our tastes and values and align with our tastes and eating habits. These ties shape not just our preferences for food but also our culinary style and dining habits, woven into our identity as chefs.

Embracing a particular food is like embarking on a journey of exploration. It involves a deep dive into the world of its ingredients, each with a distinct story and position within the food scene. It is about mastering the techniques that have been refined and refined over time techniques that form the basis of the cuisine. It also involves soaking oneself in the traditional practices that constitute the foundation of the culinary tradition, which are passed down like treasured family heirlooms. Every meal, every taste, and each technique provides an insight into the past and culture it was derived from. From the humble beginnings in street foods, when every bite is a celebration of the creativity and resourcefulness of a nation and the sophisticated techniques of high-end cuisine, where art and precision meet each aspect of food, it adds depth and a sense of richness to the culinary heritage of our country.

The appeal of a particular kind of food is its ability to create a narrative, take us away to another location and time, and bring us closer to something greater than us. It's a celebration of the diversity of our world and the common humanity that unites us all. When we explore and embrace one particular food, we broaden our horizons in food and increase our understanding and appreciation for our world and its diverse cultures.

The dining experience is an interdisciplinary aspect of our culinary culture, which includes not just the food but also the atmosphere as well as the service and overall ambiance that create memories of meals. The place where we eat our meals, such as a warm home-cooked meal, an enticing street food stand, or a sophisticated fine dining establishment, significantly influences our food preferences and determines our food-related experience.

Casual dining, characterized by its casual ambiance and comfort food, brings warmth and comfort. The atmosphere is about enjoying simple, nutritious food in a relaxed setting, focusing on the satisfaction of eating and the joy of sharing meals. It's a place where the culinary gimmicks are put aside, and the primary focus is on the genuine and frank enjoyment of food. Casual dining connects with those seeking sanctuary from everyday life's stress. It offers a warm embrace with familiar foods and a comfortable environment.

In contrast, fine dining is the highest level of culinary art. It's a symphony of textures, flavors, and presentation; every detail is carefully orchestrated. The atmosphere in the dining room of a fine establishment is infused with class. The service is distinguished by attention to detail and precision, and the food is a testimony to the highest standards of food preparation. Fine dining goes beyond the simple dining experience as it's an entire experience that involves all of the senses, leaving an irresistible impression on the person dining. It's a quest into the unusual, where every dish is a tale, each taste is a note that plays in harmony, and every presentation is a visual masterpiece.

Furthermore, the kind of dining experience isn't limited to the dividing line between elegant and casual. Many other types of dining experiences help shape our cultural identity. For instance, the family-style shared dining style, which sees dishes shared and tossed through the tables, promotes unity and warmth. A fun and interactive experience at cooking classes or the chef's table, in which guests are encouraged to participate in each step, provides more appreciation for how to cook and the kitchen's expertise.

The Other Five Senses

Cultural influences and local traditions determine the dining experience. Like a traditional tea ceremony, the traditional tea ceremony isn't just about tea but a ceremony that embodies a belief system of aesthetics, hospitality, and a sense of mindfulness. Like communal dining during a traditional Ethiopian meal, where diners are served food on one plate with injera serving as a utensil staple and staple, it is a memorable culinary experience that expresses the cultural values of sharing and community.

In the contemporary culinary landscape, the idea of dining is constantly evolving. Food trucks, pop-up restaurants, and supper clubs offer innovative dining experiences that challenge the conventional ideas of what a typical meal could be. These new dining options allow chefs to experiment and enable customers to explore new culinary horizons. They signify a shift to more exciting, dynamic, and experiential dining focused on creativity and innovation in making memorable experiences.

The dining experience is an essential aspect of our culinary identity that shapes our tastes and perceptions and forms part of our gastronomic narrative. Whether it's the comfort of a casual dinner, the elegance of fine dining, or the uniqueness of an alternative dining model, every experience adds a new dimension to our identity as a chef that enriches our experience with food and enhances our appreciation of the fine art of dining.

As we seek to define and develop our culinary identity, our choices influence the gastronomic persona we want to portray. Making decisions requires an enthralling blend of reflection, aspiration, pragmatism, and reflection. It's not simply about selecting ingredients or recipes. It's about aligning our food choices with the more fundamental aspects of our identities, values, and aspirations.

The process of developing a cohesive culinary identity starts with a deep examination. This requires deeply examining our preferences, tastes, culture, and experiences. It's about exploring these sensory influences that have defined our palates, the flavors that trigger memories, and dishes that resonate with us. This inner reflection process helps lay the foundation for making educated choices that reflect our authentic gourmet selves.

When we have a good grasp of our culinary heritage, the Next step is to express our goals. What do we want as our identity as chefs? Are we attracted to the rustic appeal of traditional recipes, or do we strive to expand the boundaries of modern food? Determining our goals will provide a direction that guides us through our food journey and our choices toward fulfilling our gastronomic goals.

Aspiration drives our culinary dreams, but pragmatism ensures our decisions are rooted in reality. It is about considering practical limitations like the availability of ingredients, cooking abilities, and lifestyle considerations. For instance, someone aspiring to live a healthier lifestyle should consider the nutritional implications of their choices in food and the possibility of sustaining a specific diet. Pragmatism is the art of finding the right balance between our ideals and the reality of our daily lives.

Decision-Making in Action: Crafting Our Culinary Identity

- **Ingredient Selection:** The selection of ingredients is an essential decision that reflects our culinary style. We can choose organic products, exotic spices, or local-sourced meats; every ingredient reflects our preferences and values.
- **Techniques for Cooking:** The methods we use in the kitchen help define our culinary style. From the slow and

meditative cooking of a dish to the quick and fiery stir-fry, every method gives an individual flavor to our food items.

- **Disposition and Plating:** How we present our food reflects our personalities as chefs. A simple, well-organized platter demonstrates a love of elegance and simplicity, and a substantial, hearty serving suggests a more generous and comforting style.

- **Cultural Influences:** Releasing the tradition of our food culture or incorporating elements of other cultures into our food is a choice that enhances your culinary experience. It's an acknowledgment of cultural diversity and the interconnectedness of our global culinary landscape.

Ethics and sustainability Many people use sustainable and ethically-sourced food items, an integral part of their culinary culture. It's a pledge to sustainable stewardship of the environment and social responsibility.

It's crucial to understand that our food identity isn't static. It develops as we discover new tastes, learn new techniques, and gain new knowledge. This dynamic aspect of the food culture means that our choices must be able to change. We must be open to leaving our familiar zones and accepting the change. It's an ongoing process of improvement, where every step brings us closer to the food identity we want.

Making the right decisions in the context of what we would like our identity as a chef to be is a complex, multifaceted process. It requires a profound understanding of the roots of our cuisine, a clear idea of our dreams, and a practical way to translate those aspirations into reality. Every decision, from the ingredients we select to our methods, can be a foundational element that creates our culinary identity. It's a process of exploration, self-expression, and creativity to develop an authentic and unique culinary identity. Truly and unique to us.

The consequences can be long-lasting and complex if we aren't honest about ourselves, our identity, and our food preferences. Dishonesty about oneself can cause a gap between the real us and the personas we present. This can result in many social, psychological, and even gastronomic effects. One of the main effects of this lack of transparency is the loss of self-awareness. If we're not honest about who we are, we can lose touch with our needs, beliefs, values, and hopes. This may manifest as an eerie feeling of disorientation because our authentic selves do not guide us but rather by the expectations of others or social norms. Our food identity can cause us to adopt food preferences or cooking methods that don't appeal to our tastes, resulting in unsatisfied and enjoying our culinary experiences.

The inconsistency between our authentic self and the image we portray can cause emotional turmoil and internal conflict in turn affecting our professional life and the food we serve. The continuous effort to create an appearance that doesn't match our true self could be stressful and exhausting, leading to depression, anxiety, or feelings of being unauthentic. In the world of cooking, it could be reflected as a reluctance to experiment with new cuisines or flavors because of fear of judgment, which can hinder creativity and personal development.

Social relationships also suffer because of the insecurity. Authentic connections are built upon trust and transparency. Friendship and understanding can be hindered if we're not transparent about who we are. When it comes to food, this could be a reason to miss an opportunity to share memorable food experiences with friends or to share food preferences and tastes. A lack of authenticity with oneself could hinder your personal growth and development. If we're not aligned with who we are and our true selves, we could be unable to discover new interests, acquire new abilities, or pursue interests that could enhance our lives. Regarding our culinary identity, this might mean that we miss out on learning new cooking techniques, cuisines, or ingredients that can increase our knowledge of food and appreciation for food.

In the field of professionalism, particularly for those working in the culinary field, having a false perception of your culinary style could have grave consequences. It could lead to an inconsistency between the style of food served by chefs and their clients and could affect the performance and image of their restaurant. In addition, it can hinder creativity and originality as chefs may be compelled to follow styles or trends instead of developing their unique vision of food.

Untruthfulness about yourself can have long-term effects on our general well-being and happiness. Being in tune with our authentic selves is the key to a satisfying and meaningful life. If we don't acknowledge our true identity to avoid being genuine, we forfeit the chance to live life wholly and fully. In terms of culinary, accepting our true identity as a chef lets us feel the joy and delight of food in a genuinely personal and satisfying manner. The consequences of not being authentic about ourselves, how we present ourselves, and our identity as a cook are profound and sweeping. It impacts our mental health as well as our relationships, personal development, as well as our satisfaction with food. Honesty and authenticity are crucial to living a fulfilled and fulfilling culinary journey.

Dishonesty, a deviation from reality, has far-reaching implications across all aspects of our lives and the world of cuisine. In food identity, dishonesty may manifest in various forms, including misrepresenting ingredients or appropriating and not acknowledging traditional dishes. This study explores the consequences of dishonesty and explains its effect on the integrity of the individual, culture, and confidence.

The foundation of a chef's identity is personal integrity, an obligation to be honest, and authenticity when it comes to the expressions one uses in cooking. Infidelity, whether due to mislabeled ingredients or exaggerating the skills of a chef, is a breach of the integrity of the chef. It can cause a disconnect between the real chef and the image he presents to the public. The lapse of integrity can result in a loss of self-esteem and satisfaction since the awards received are based on appearance rather than actual ability or hard work.

Culinary identity is entwined with heritage and culture. Every dish acts as a symbol of the culture's past, customs, and cultural values. Dishonesty in the form of cultural appropriation--adopting elements of a culture without proper understanding or respect--can dilute and misrepresent that culture's culinary heritage. It removes dishes from their significance and context, making them merely exotic novelty items for commercial profit. This not only devalues the origins of the cuisine but also hinders the consumers from having the chance to truly experience the richness and variety of the global culinary tradition.

Trust is a crucial element in the relationships between chefs and their customers. If chefs or food manufacturers are not honest about the source and quality of their items, they undermine the trust of their customers. For instance, using products made in factories as artisanal or using less expensive substitutes while asserting authenticity could lead to consumer discontent. Once trust is lost, rebuilding can be difficult, leading to lasting damage to the chef's or restaurant's reputation.

Untruthfulness in the kitchen could severely threaten people's health and safety. Incorrectly labeling allergens or failing to declare the presence of certain ingredients can cause serious harm to people who have dietary restrictions or are allergic. In addition, shady practices like using expired or contaminated ingredients could result in foodborne illness, damaging the establishment's image and putting public health at risk.

Involving in fraudulent practices could cause legal consequences such as lawsuits, fines, and the loss of licenses. The regulatory bodies and consumer protection regulations are in place to ensure that food items are correctly depicted and are safe to consume. Infractions of these laws not only result in sanctions for violations of the law but also indicate an absence of moral responsibility and can undermine the credibility of the chef establishment or professional.

In the context of a culinary identity, it can have significant consequences beyond the individual, affecting the community's cultural heritage, consumer trust, public health, and the legal status of a business. Honesty and integrity are not just a matter of pride in oneself but a responsibility to protect the experience's authenticity and security. Therefore, it is crucial for professionals in the culinary arts field to promote transparency and authenticity in their food and to ensure that their identity is an authentic representation of the values they hold, as well as their expertise and respect for the many facets of world culinary styles.

In the culinary arts, where perfection and precision are valued above all, vulnerability may seem odd. For me, embracing vulnerability has transformed his life professionally and personally. My life story sheds light on how vulnerability can provide authenticity and strength, shaping the identity of one's chef in profound ways.

According to Brene Brown, vulnerability refers to the ability to come out and be observed, to take risks, and to risk emotional vulnerability. For me, this meant taking a step outside the safety zone of traditional practices in the kitchen and embracing my distinctive style and vision. It was about overcoming the fear of judgment or criticism and committing to his passions and culinary instincts.

This vulnerability was evident in my professional cooking style and menu design. I began to explore unorthodox flavors in the kitchen based on my personal experiences and feelings. I began to enliven his food by telling stories. Each dish becomes a canvas to express my artistic expression. My authenticity was a hit, and my food's authenticity and passion attracted my customers. My willingness to share this vulnerability stood out in a crowded field, establishing my reputation as a chef with an individual culinary style.

Vulnerability played an essential part in my style of leadership. In a field typically associated with high-pressure and rough outsides, I intentionally created an atmosphere of trust and encouragement. I encouraged my staff to communicate their thoughts and ideas and created a place that allowed collaboration and creativity to thrive. This strategy enhanced the team's performance and created an environment of camaraderie and confidence, evident in the high quality of the team's work.

Accepting vulnerability helped me to be more in touch with others and myself. I became more attentive to my own feelings and how they affected my cooking, which led to an empathetic and thoughtful approach to my work. The emotional awareness of my work enhanced his cooking by adding depth and sophistication to my menus. The vulnerability helped strengthen connections with my mentors, peers, and patrons. Through transparency about my struggles and achievements, I developed relationships based on respect and mutual trust. These connections gave me invaluable help and feedback, contributing to my progress as a chef and an individual.

The effect of vulnerability on my identity as a chef can be seen in my style of cooking development. In time, my recipes have evolved into more evocative and personal, telling an account of my life. Being vulnerable has been the hallmark characteristic of my culinary art.

My experiences highlight the significance of vulnerability in developing one's identity as a chef. It shows how being vulnerable can bring more authenticity, creativity, and connections at the table and in other areas. For aspiring chefs or culinary professionals, my story is a reminder that being vulnerable can lead to identifying and defining one's unique culinary voice.

Recognizing our influences is crucial since they significantly shape our gastronomic preferences, decisions, and lifestyles. Our influences are diverse and encompass family traditions, cultural heritage, personal experiences, and even the larger socio-economic context. Knowing how these influences affect our lives can give us a profound insight into our identity as a foodie that influences our food choices and relationships to gastronomy.

The cultural heritage of our country is an essential influence on our food culture. The dishes of the past, as well as cooking methods and the food items of our ancestors, provide the basis for our culinary preferences. For instance, someone who hails from the Mediterranean region might prefer olive oil and fresh vegetables and seafood, which reflects the cuisine of that region. A person of Asian heritage might be drawn to rice-based dishes, soy sauce, and a myriad of spices that reflect the cuisine traditions of their roots. These cultural influences determine our food preferences and our views of comfort food, meals for celebrations, and our everyday eating practices.

Family traditions play an integral part in shaping our food identity. The recipes handed over generations, the rituals accompanying cooking, and the sharing of meals with family members enormously contribute to our culinary recipes. These customs create a feeling of continuity and belonging, connecting us to our heritage and helping to establish the foundation of our food preferences. For instance, the family habit of preparing pies to celebrate special occasions could instill an ongoing love of baking within a person and influence their food preferences in the adult years.

Personal experiences, such as travel, education, and experiments, can be instrumental in shaping our food preferences. The exposure to various food items, as well as ingredients and cooking techniques, broadens our gastronomic perspectives and affects our choices in food. For example, someone who has traveled extensively through Southeast Asia may desire aromatic, spicy food items and incorporate elements from Thai or Vietnamese dishes into their selection. In the same way, culinary education can help better understand various cooking methods and flavor profiles, leading to an enhanced and varied culinary style.

The socio-economic context can play a crucial role in determining our food preferences. Factors such as the availability of ingredients, the status of the economy, and regional trends can affect our choices. For instance, a person who lives in a coastal region might have access to fresh seafood, which makes it a staple of their diet. However, financial constraints could hinder an individual's ability to explore exotic ingredients or eat at high-end restaurants, affecting their food choices and experiences.

The influences that shape our food choices influence different aspects of our gastronomic life. They influence our taste preferences and shape our palates, making our decisions about food items and recipes. They influence our cooking style by determining whether we prefer rustic, simple, or more elaborate gourmet meals. These influences influence our eating habits, ranging from the type of restaurant we go to to how we host guests at home.

Accepting and understanding these influences can help create a more authentic and satisfying food identity. It lets us connect to our heritage, explore new territories of gastronomy, and develop a distinctive style of cooking that reflects the uniqueness of our experiences and culture. It also gives us an appreciation for and confidence in food choices, allowing us to share our food culture with the world and revel in the variety of cuisine.

Understanding our influences and recognizing their influence on us is essential to creating a diverse and rich food-related identity. It doesn't matter if it's the tradition of our culture that forms the basis, the family traditions that provide continuity, personal experiences that expand our perspectives, and the socio-economic context that shapes our options. Each aspect plays an essential part in defining our culinary self. When we acknowledge and embrace the influences of these factors, we will be able to navigate through the world of food with a greater sense of self-awareness and purpose, enhancing our dining experience and developing an increased connection to our food choices.

Developing a solid sense of self is connected to developing leadership skills, specifically within the domain of identity in the culinary field. The relationship between self-awareness and leadership is highlighted by the need for chefs and other professionals in the field not just to master their art but also to be able to inspire, guide, and influence their team members and the larger culinary world.

In the ever-changing atmosphere of the culinary industry, having a clear self-awareness is the foundation upon which leadership abilities are founded. This self-awareness is based on a profound awareness of one's strengths, weaknesses, values, and passions. For an experienced chef, this may be recognizing their distinctive cooking style, approach to flavors and ingredients, and philosophy regarding the food industry and host. A clear understanding of oneself is essential, as it guides one's decision-making process and shapes one's expression of creativity and how one interacts with others.

Creating a sense of self-worth fosters authenticity, a valuable trait for leadership. A true leader are authentic, open, transparent, and committed to their ideals and values, which creates confidence and respect from the team members. In the realm of culinary, authentic chefs lead by example, adhering to their culinary philosophy as they respect the traditions and trends of the culinary world. This authenticity gives faith in the company's leadership and creates a sense of integrity and honesty in the kitchen.

Self-awareness increases emotional intelligence, which is a crucial aspect of effective leadership. Emotional intelligence is the capacity to recognize and manage your emotions and other people's emotional state. Professional chefs with high emotional intelligence can manage conflicts, stress, and interpersonal tension in a stressful kitchen with grace and understanding. They can offer assistance and motivation to their staff, create favorable working conditions, and establish solid and cooperative relationships.

Confidence in oneself allows the chef to express their values and vision transparently, which is vital to lead a team to achieve the same purpose. Clarity of vision is essential in the world of food, and a shared dedication to innovation, excellence, and customer satisfaction is critical to success. Chefs who articulate their culinary vision and goals effectively can motivate their staff to share these values, pursue their work passionately, and strive to achieve excellence.

Developing an identity develops resilience, a trait essential for leadership in the culinary field. Life for a professional chef is rife with challenges, ranging from the high pressure of providing service to the relentless desire for perfection. Chefs who have confidence in themselves have the strength to endure setbacks, learn from mistakes, and persevere regardless of the odds. This resilience is not just an example for their staff; it also helps ensure the longevity of their leadership and the sustainability of their culinary efforts.

A well-defined identity allows the chef to appreciate and harness diversity, an essential aspect of leadership in a world of cuisine. Knowing one's cultural background and identity as a chef helps one understand and embrace different perspectives, tastes, and methods. The willingness to embrace diversity encourages innovation, enhances the dining experience, and fosters greater inclusion within the kitchen and in the broader community of chefs.

The process of self-discovery, as well as the personal growth that comes with self-confidence, is also a source of passion and creative thinking. Chefs at peace with their self-image tend to explore risk, experiment, and expand the limits of culinary excellence. Their enthusiasm and innovative spirit can be infectious and inspire the team to think of new concepts, explore tastes, and strive to be the best at what they do.

The growth of a sense of self is a crucial element of leadership in the culinary sector. It is the basis for authenticity, emotional intelligence, open communication, resilience, creative thinking, and diversity. All of these are vital for effective leadership. When chefs and professionals build their self-esteem and self-confidence, they strengthen their own personal culinary style and motivate and inspire others around them, resulting in an ever-expanding, vibrant culinary scene.

Chefs' leadership in the kitchen is the foundation of a culinary identity. It shapes any culinary venture's character, efficiency, and ultimate achievement. The leadership of a kitchen isn't just concerned with authoritative oversight. It is a complex orchestration of abilities, vision, and interpersonal relationships that culminate in the creation of culinary excellence.

Successful kitchen leadership's core is the capacity to motivate and inspire an entire team. An individual leader with enthusiasm for cooking and a desire to achieve excellence could inspire the same enthusiasm among the team members. This is vital in a workplace that is as hectic and stressful as the professional kitchen. The chef's passion can act as a catalyst to transform mundane tasks into moments of excellence and transform challenges into growth opportunities.

The chef's leadership is crucial in creating a culture based on collaboration and respect. The kitchen is a melting pot of different talents and personalities; each brings a unique flavor to the overall experience. An experienced leader manages this variety with aplomb, creating an environment where each team member feels valued and respected. This diversity boosts morale and facilitates the free flow of ideas that result in greater creativity and a more rich cooking output.

Another crucial aspect of kitchen management is the capacity to keep calm and focus under stress. The kitchen is fluid, and unexpected challenges occur frequently. The ability of a leader to remain calm and focused when confronted with these difficulties determines the mood of the whole team. This ensures that any obstacles are handled efficiently and with precision and provides the highest quality of the dining experience.

In addition, the leadership of cooking extends beyond the management of resources and maintaining quality standards. Leaders must have an eye for detail and ensure that each ingredient, technique, and meal is prepared to meet the highest standards of excellence. The attention to detail takes the dining experience from the mundane to the extraordinary. Furthermore, a responsible leader will ensure a sustainable utilization of resources while balancing business needs with ethical and environmental obligations.

The impact of leadership within the kitchen is also felt outside the immediate setting of food. It affects the overall food and beverage identity of the establishment and its place within the world of food. A strong leader defines the restaurant's food philosophy by specifying how it approaches the food industry, its commitment to innovation, and its involvement with traditional cuisine. This leadership defines the restaurant's style and distinctiveness, separating it from a competitive food scene.

Leadership at the table is at the heart of a culinary identity. It's the factor that inspires innovation, sustains the highest standards, and creates an environment of collaboration and respect. A kitchen that is not led effectively is like a dish with no seasoning. It lacks flavor and cohesion. A kitchen governed by a creative, skilled, and compassionate leader is an area where dreams of culinary excellence are fulfilled, every dish is a testimony to the fine art of food preparation, and where the uniqueness of food is preserved, honored, and raised to new levels.

The path from a cook to being a chef is characterized by the development of specific qualities of leadership that are vital in the world of food. In the kitchen, leadership isn't just about managing a team or preparing menus; it's about motivating others, setting high standards, and creating an environment in which creativity in the kitchen can flourish. These traits are not just what defines a great leader but are essential in making a cook a more skilled Chef over time and ultimately creating their own culinary identity.

The Other Five Senses

A successful chef has a clear view of their kitchen and cuisine. They can anticipate the latest trends in food, create new dishes, and make an example for others to follow. This thinking is essential when a cook is transitioning to being a chef since it helps them create a distinct style of cooking that makes them stand out from other chefs.

Passion for the culinary arts and a commitment to their craft are the characteristics of a successful chef who is a leader in the kitchen. Their unwavering dedication keeps them striving to develop, test, and challenge the limits of cooking that is traditional. As a chef, their passion and determination can be infectious, inspiring them to develop their talents and push for the highest quality in their culinary dishes.

The ability to communicate effectively is essential to leadership success in the kitchen. A great leader communicates their vision, communicates clear directions, and gives constructive feedback. This creates an open atmosphere of dialogue and collaboration, which allows cooks to grow, learn, and improve their skills and perspectives on food.

A successful leader has a high degree of emotional intelligence. This lets them be aware of and manage their own emotions, as well as the feelings of their staff. This is crucial in the stressful work atmosphere of the kitchen, where stress levels get high. A cook needs an effective leader who maintains calm and offers support in times of stress, which is crucial for their professional growth and overall well-being.

The culinary world constantly changes, and a successful leader shows resilience and flexibility in facing challenges. They can handle the challenges that come with it, whether managing supply chain issues, adjusting to changes in dietary preferences, or handling an emergency in the kitchen. A cook's observation and learning from the leader's resilience can give them confidence and resiliency, allowing them to manage the constantly changing nature of the business.

A great chef is also a teacher and mentor. They spend time training, guiding, and encouraging their chefs' skills. By sharing their knowledge and experience, they aid cooks improve their skills, develop their techniques, and gain more understanding of the culinary art. This mentoring is vital in transitioning a cook to a chef since it gives them the base and confidence to lead and innovate independently.

A successful chef is a leader who strives to achieve culinary excellence and promotes creativity. They set the bar high regarding food quality, presentation, and creativity in their team, encouraging them to go above and beyond expectations. As a chef being under the direction of a chef who is committed to excellence and innovation gives them the chance to push their boundaries and be a part of the development of the menu as well as the distinctiveness of the restaurant's cuisine.

Leaders who are successful understand the importance of collaboration and team building within the kitchen. They create a sense of unity, respect, and support between the team members. A collaborative work environment is vital to the development of a cook because it enables the cook to take lessons from fellow cooks to share their ideas, collaborate, and collaborate toward an end purpose.

The qualities of a successful leader in the food world include various aspects and go beyond just technical abilities. They mix creative thinking, passion, emotional intelligence, communication, perseverance, mentorship excellence, collaboration, and mentorship. These characteristics indicate a successful leader and play a significant part in the progress towards becoming a better cook. As a cook grows to become a professional chef, qualities are embedded in their identity as a chef, forming their cooking style and how they interact with their team, and general contribution to culinary art.

Self-awareness is a critical component of personal growth. It requires a thorough knowledge of our strengths, weaknesses, preferences, and personal values. This process of reflection helps us navigate our professional lives with clarity and focus. If we are aware of our capabilities and limitations, we can make educated decisions that align with our aspirations and goals.

Self-awareness also helps us recognize our emotional triggers and control our responses in the workplace. It helps us maintain calm in stressful situations, effectively communicate with colleagues, and develop strong relationships with colleagues. By understanding ourselves, we can find areas for expansion and improvement, leading to constant improvement and higher satisfaction at work.

Acceptance is a crucial aspect of personal growth. It requires embracing our uniqueness and aspects of us that we may consider imperfection. It is liberating because it lets us free from the burden of trying to conform to certain molds. Instead, we are honest and authentic to ourselves, which is an essential quality to have in any professional environment. Genuineness in the workplace builds trust and respect among coworkers. If we're honest and honest, colleagues tend to share their thoughts and work effectively. It also helps us connect with our work more deeply, leading to tremendous enthusiasm and dedication.

In addition, recognizing our unique strengths allows us to maximize our strengths and overcome our weaknesses. It is possible to focus on what we excel at, ask for help, or delegate tasks in areas where we might not perform to our best. This can lead to greater efficiency and effectiveness and a more accessible and more fulfilling professional life.

Being able to accept ourselves will have a significant influence on our choices for careers. When we understand what we love to do and the areas we excel in, we choose career paths that align with our interests and talents. This will increase job satisfaction because we will be more likely to enjoy working and feel inspired to succeed. Self-awareness also allows us to establish realistic goals for ourselves and establish an outline of how to reach these goals. We can determine the skills and experience needed to obtain and make informed decisions regarding our professional growth. This approach to career planning can increase the chances of success and long-term satisfaction within the field we choose to work in.

The way we perceive and accept ourselves can affect our relationships at work. Self-awareness allows us to communicate better, manage conflict constructively, and build a positive relationship with our colleagues. We know our communication style and can adapt to communicate well with various people. Accepting ourselves is also about being aware of our emotional responses and triggers. This knowledge helps us manage workplace situations by utilizing emotional intelligence creating an inclusive and respectful workplace. Being authentic and considerate makes it possible to build solid professional relationships that improve collaboration.

Self-aware leaders who are genuine are more likely to gain the respect and trust of their colleagues. They can lead by example, and they are honest and sincere in their commitment to the well-being of their team. This type of leadership creates an atmosphere of positivity and trust that makes employees feel appreciated and energized to give their highest.

Self-aware leaders are better equipped to deal with the difficulties of leadership. They recognize their weaknesses, admit their mistakes, and learn from their experiences. The willingness to grow and develop makes them adept and flexible leaders capable of leading their teams through changes and uncertainty.

Understanding and accepting our worthiness is essential to professional achievement. It impacts all aspects of our professional daily lives, from the decisions we make to the relationships we establish and the style of leadership that we choose to adopt. When we are aware, genuine, and authentic, we can traverse our professional path with confidence, resiliency, and satisfaction. The process of self-awareness and acceptance continues to evolve and is constantly changing. While we discover more about ourselves and appreciate our uniqueness, we can find our potential to achieve the ultimate success in our lives, both in our professional and personal lives.

The road to professional success depends on our perception of our self-awareness. It's a path that requires more than just skills and experience but also an awareness of oneself. The understanding of our self is the basis of our identity. And guides us in making choices that align with our authentic selves.

Self-awareness begins by recognizing our strengths. These are the traits and talents that distinguish us and the abilities we are naturally good at. These are our strengths in the workplace and the tools we employ to find our niche and be successful in the fields we choose to specialize in. By recognizing and harnessing our strengths, we set ourselves to be successful and fulfilled. It is equally important to be aware of our weak points. This is the area that we may struggle, abilities that don't come so quickly to us. Recognizing our weaknesses isn't about dwelling on our weaknesses but our shortcomings. It helps us look for opportunities to grow, develop, and create an overall professional profile.

Knowing our personal preferences is another essential element of self-awareness. It's about understanding the type of work that stimulates us, the environments where we thrive, and the jobs we enjoy. This information helps us decide on a career path that aligns with our passions and interests and ensures that our careers aren't just fulfilling and enjoyable. They are the moral guide that guides our professional life. They are the values we believe in and guide our actions and decisions. Knowing our values helps us make sense of ethical dilemmas, make trusted decisions, and establish an image of professionalism that is in line with our values.

The process of understanding oneself is never-ending. It requires continuous contemplation and reflection. As we develop and change in our lives, so do our strengths, weaknesses, preferences, and beliefs. Being aware of these changes helps ensure that our lives in the workplace remain in tune with our authentic selves. Self-awareness is also about understanding our emotions and their impact on our work. It's about recognizing our triggers, managing stress, and using the power of our feelings to create strong relationships with colleagues. When we are aware of the emotions of our lives, we can manage the challenges of work with ease and strength.

A different aspect of self-understanding is understanding our style of learning. We can be auditory, visual, or kinesthetic. Understanding how we process information is a great way to improve our professional growth. It lets us tailor our learning experiences to meet our preferences, making learning more efficient and enjoyable. The self-awareness factor extends to the style of communication, too. Being aware of how we speak, listen, and react to feedback is crucial in the workplace. It allows us to effectively communicate, build relationships between colleagues, and constructively solve disputes.

Understanding how we work is a further important factor. Are we morning-lovers or night early risers? Are we able to prefer pressure or prefer a more steady pace? Understanding our working habits can help us maximize our efficiency and manage our time efficiently. Self-awareness is also about understanding the impact we have on other people. It's about recognizing how our attitudes, behavior, and actions impact our coworkers and the working environment. This understanding will allow us to positively contribute to our workplace environment and create a culture of collaboration and respect.

The path to success in the workplace is not only about external accomplishments. It's also about personal growth. Understanding our strengths allows us to manage our career paths with purpose and a sense of authenticity. We can make decisions that are not only solid but also profoundly satisfying. Self-awareness is the basis that allows us to create the professional life we want to live that is productive, meaningful, and true to who we are.

CHAPTER FOUR

A Sense of Timing

Timing functions as the silent conductor of the kitchen, harmonizing a symphony of tastes that awaken textures, flavors, and aromas that gracefully traverse the palate. When a main course is grilled at the precise temperature, a gentle simmer transforms vegetables into a delectable stew—a delicate equilibrium between the crispness and tenderness of a perfectly baked pastry. Within the intricate tapestry of culinary craft, timing assumes a pivotal role in guiding chefs through the elaborate choreography of creation, ensuring that each dish attains its zenith.

Take, for instance, an egg, which is an essential ingredient. When handled by an experienced chef, the egg can be transformed into an array of culinary delights, ranging from silky hollandaise sauce to fluffy and light egg omelets. However, mastering the process of cooking eggs requires skill and precision. Just a few minutes too long in the oven, and the perfectly runny yolk turns solid and tasteless. One too long time, and the eggs remain undercooked, leading to an unsatisfactory texture. It's an intricate balance that distinguishes eggs that aren't appropriately cooked from a truly outstanding dish.

Timing is also a crucial part of the creation of flavor. For instance, that process is called caramelization. When sugars get heated, they undergo a sophisticated chemical reaction, which produces the most delicious, nutty taste and a rich golden hue. However, achieving the proper caramelization requires careful consideration of the timing and the temperature. Too high a temperature can cause the sugars to burn and impart a bitter taste to the food. Insufficient heat and the caramelization process slows and pays off in a dull taste. It's a delicate line chefs must tread, and when done correctly and with perfection, the payoff is fantastic.

Additionally, timing depends on our senses, affecting how we feel about scent, taste, and hearing. Please take a moment to consider the rising anticipation as the scent of fresh-baked bread wafts through the air, signaling that it's time to savor an icy slice of bread slathered in butter. The satisfying crunch of an exquisitely seared steak signifies that it's been cooked to the highest standards. These taste cues aren't simply random, and they're created by chefs who know that timing plays a crucial role when making memorable dining experiences.

However, the timing of food in the world goes beyond the kitchen; it covers the wider culture of traditions, seasonal variations, and personal tastes that influence our tastes in food. From meal timings to the choice of ingredients according to seasonal availability, Every aspect of the food experience is affected by the time of day.

This chapter will dive deeper into the science of timing within the world of food, explore its diverse facets, and discover the secrets to the art of mastering this vital ability. From the cooking technique to the importance of culture for meals, we'll explore the role that timing plays in each aspect of our food landscape. So, join us as we explore the complex time-based world of food, where every second counts and every moment is celebrated.

The art of timing in the kitchen is similar to orchestrating a harmoning, in which each element has to work together to create a masterpiece. It's more than the simple process of cooking. It's an

The Other Five Senses

intricate dance that involves all of the senses and culminates in an experience of sensory that goes beyond the mundane. Timing is crucial. It goes way beyond just ensuring that the food is cooked perfectly. It affects all aspects of the dining experience, from the anticipation of the first bite to the flavors that remain in the mouth long after the meal is finished.

Take, for sample, the process of searing the steak. The timing should be precise. If it's too short and the steak is undercooked. If it is too long, the meat will be dry and tough. It's an artful balance that requires care and a thorough grasp of how heat alters ingredients. The timing of adding spices and herbs can be the key to making a difference in a dish, improving the flavor, and elevating it from ordinary to outstanding.

Timing in the kitchen isn't just about cooking food, it's essential to know when to serve it. An adequately timed meal can give an atmosphere of anticipation and excitement, enhancing enjoyment. Imagine the pleasure of cutting into a perfectly cooked steak when the juices begin to run or of the joy of breaking open an ice cream brulee and revealing the custard's creamy layer beneath the sugar crust that has been caramelized. These culinary moments can be achieved through precise timing.

Timing plays a vital part in the appearance of food. The appearance of food can be significantly enhanced by placing every ingredient in the dish. Adding a garnish in the final moments of serving could grant an extra splash of freshness and color, whereas the sauce drizzle right before serving could add an extra touch of class. This way, the timing is an integral component of the creation process, allowing chefs to showcase their creativity through the arrangement of their ingredients.

Beyond the realms of sight and taste, timing can also affect our other senses. The scent of a meal that is afloat in the air could trigger memories and stir emotion, creating a feeling of anticipation that enhances the experience of dining. The sound of simmering hot meat or bubbling sauce may add to the experience by adding an element of excitement and drama to the dining experience. The texture of food is influenced by the cooking time, and an ideal balance of crispness and tenderness is achieved through meticulous cooking and exact timing.

The essence of timing will be the intangible thread that holds to every aspect of the dining experience. It's the difference between a decent dinner and a truly memorable one and between a skilled cook and a renowned chef. When they understand how important timing is and hone the knowledge in this critical area, chefs can take their skills to new heights, preparing meals that satisfy the taste buds and nourish your soul. In the culinary art, timing is everything.

The rhythm of the ingredients and techniques is the underlying rhythm of culinary art. It's a delicate dance in which every move is important, each ingredient is a part of the equation and each technique has to be executed with a high degree of precision. To fully grasp the meaning that is timing within the world of food it is essential to understand the intricate relationship between these crucial ingredients.

Ingredients are the primary ingredients of every dish, with each having distinct flavor and characteristics. From the vivid hues of fresh fruits and vegetables to the rich oozing from aged cheeses the ingredients add depth and variety to the culinary dishes. However, their real power is in the way they interact with each other. Like a proportion in the ingredients have to be harmonious with each other, each note complimenting the other to form a harmonious total. Timing is essential in this coordination, deciding the accurate time you should add every ingredient into the mix as well as when to apply some heat to bring out their flavor then when they should stop the process to keep their original flavor.

Techniques, in turn, are the instruments that chefs alter ingredients in order to benefit bring their ideas to reality. From braising and sauteing, to baking and grilling every technique adds its own distinctive flavor and texture to food. However, mastering these techniques is more than merely technical knowledge; it requires an ability to judge the timing. Being aware of when you should flip delicate fish fillets in order to accomplish that perfect sear or when to whip egg whites into stiff peaks to create an airy meringue or when to take the cooking pot from the stove to prevent the sauce from forming a curdle—all these decisions depend on precise timing.

The art of timing goes far beyond the walls of the kitchen. The way we eat is affected by a multitude of external influences, such as the cultural tradition along with seasonal variations and individual preferences. The cultural traditions, for instance define the timings of meals and other rituals and influence the way we view food and dining. In certain societies, certain meals have been reserved only for certain occasions however, others are eaten everyday as part of a common food culture. Respecting and understanding these traditions is vital for chefs who want for original and meaningful dining experiences.

The seasons are also a major factor in the timing of food preparation, since ingredient availability changes according to changes in the seasons. From the tender asparagus spears of spring, to the crisp apple of autumn, seasonal produce not only gives the most delicious flavors but also sparks new dishes that showcase the bounty of nature. Chefs need to adjust their menus to the changing seasons and using seasonal ingredients at their peak of ripeness.

Our personal preferences determine our timing preferences in the kitchen that affect everything from cooking techniques to pairings with flavors. Some individuals may prefer their steak cooked to a rare state however, others prefer it cooked well. Some people may prefer the strong flavor of spicy food while some prefer subtle flavors of mild meals. Catering to individual preferences will require chefs to stay able to adapt to the different desires and tastes of their patrons by adjusting their timings and methods in accordance with their preferences.

The cultural traditions and seasonal variations profoundly influence how we view timing in the world of food. These factors provide more layers of sophistication and variety to the experience of eating that influence not just what we eat but also the time and the way we eat it. In all cultures, certain seasons have importance for the culinary practices. It doesn't matter if it's the abundance of fresh fruits and vegetables in the summer, or the comfort food staples that winter brings, the seasons determine the available ingredients and the meals that are cooked.

The cultural traditions are a major factor in determining the time of rituals and meals. In certain traditions there are meals that are scheduled for specific dates or for specific occasions, like lunch, breakfast, or dinner. These traditions usually reflect the social rules, rituals of religion and family customs. In several Middle Eastern cultures, the breaking of the fast during Ramadan is a sacred ceremony performed with reverence and reverence. In Japan the elaborate multi-course kaiseki feast is rooted in ancient traditions that mark the changing seasons.

Furthermore, celebrations of culture and festivals usually revolve around food, and the timing of events plays an important role in the celebrations. From elaborate meals at thanksgiving in the United States to the colorful market for street food that are held during Diwali in India These celebrations mark important occasions and bring people to one another through shared experiences in the kitchen. The time of these events is meticulously designed to coincide with significant dates in the calendar, making sure that the food is not just tasty, but also filled with meaning, symbolism and cultural significance.

Alongside cultural customs and customs, the seasonal rhythms of nature also affect the timing of cooking practices. Chefs and farmers alike depend on the cycles of growing, planting and harvesting to establish the time of year when certain ingredients are in their prime. The spring season is a bountiful source of fresh greens and delicate herbs and autumn brings an abundance of root vegetables as well as nutritious grains. When they align their menus to seasonal changes, cooks are able to showcase the desirable ingredients they can find and create dishes that are delicious and healthy.

Seasonal variations go beyond the mere ingredients to include the techniques used to cook and the flavors. In warmer seasons lighter, refreshing dishes are popular, with bright citrus flavors, grilled meats and fresh salads. As the temperatures cool and the temperatures drop, richer, more luxurious food is the main focus including stews and meats braised, rich soups, and delicious desserts that serve warmth and comfort. These seasonal variations do not just reflect the changing climate, but also provide the senses with a journey which connects us with the world of nature.

Traditions along with seasonal changes play an important part in determining the timeframe of our culinary practices. The ingredients that we choose to use to the food we cook along with the traditions we follow the timing of events is interspersed into our dining experiences. When we embrace these traditions and respecting the seasonal rhythms and the seasons, we can prepare dishes that nourish our body, but also nourish the soul, encouraging an increased connection with your food as well as the traditions that create it.

Timing plays the subtle role of guiding the ensemble of flavors in the realm of food. It transcends mere culinary practice, instead crafting an immersive encounter that engages all senses. Delving into the complexities of culinary timing unveils its multifaceted influence on how we perceive taste, sight, smell, and even sound. Within the culinary domain, it embodies a delicate interplay between the chef's precision and intuition. Mastery lies in discerning the opportune moments to apply heat, introduce ingredients, or allow the dish to rest. Each choice reverberates through the final outcome, shaping the dish's essence through its flavor, texture, and aroma.

Think about the art of grilling the steak. There's an important distinction between properly prepared steak and one which is too cooked is a matter of seconds. One second longer on the grill and the meat will be tender and juicy to dry and tough. To master the timing, you need to pay close concentration and quick reflexes and knowing precisely what time to turn the meat over and the perfect time to remove it from the grill.

The Other Five Senses

Timing goes beyond the moment and requires a lot of the ability to be patient and foresight. For instance, consider how to marinate. Allowing the ingredients to marinate for the appropriate duration of time could make a huge differences in the flavor of your dish. If it's just an hour or overnight the timing needs to be precise in order to accomplish the desired level of flavor.

In baking the timing of the bake is crucial as well. From the time the ingredients are incorporated until the time when they are put in the oven each second is important. Overbaking a cake could cause dry, crumbly appearance, and under baking causes it to be dry in the middle. This is a delicate process which requires careful monitoring and tweaks as needed. Timing is also a key aspect when it comes to the appearance of food. The timing of when to serve and serve will enhance the experience of dining, generating an atmosphere of anticipation as well as excitement. Imagine a flawlessly timed unveiling when a cloche is lifted to reveal an enticing hot dish that is that is bursting with flavor and aroma. The timing is a feast for the senses and invites guests to enjoy each moment with excitement.

Alongside the smell and taste Timing influences our perception of touch and sight. The appeal of food is enhanced when the ingredients are cooked perfectly with vibrant colors and the textures appealing. The texture of the dish, whether it is smooth, soft or smooth is the result of a precise time in the cooking process and dish preparation. Even sound is a factor in timing the food. The sizzle of onions striking the hot pan, or an explosion of sugar caramelized the soft rumble of steam that escapes from freshly baked loaves of bread – each sound signals a signal that helps guide the cooking process and indicates how to regulate the temperature or when food is ready to serve.

Mastering your timing skills is all about creating a sharp sense of awareness. It's an additional *sense* that helps guide each step of cooking. It's about the ability to develop intuition through experience, and a sense of knowing whether a food item is properly cooked or requires more time. It's about being in tune with the rhythm of your kitchen, letting go of its pace, and allowing inspiration to flow.

As we continue to study the subject of the timing of food preparation Let's not forget the importance of experimentation and practice. Through trials and errors that chefs develop their skills and learn from every failure and success during the course of. Although there are recipes and guidelines to follow but true mastery is the result of a profound knowledge of the ingredients techniques, ingredients, and delicate details of timing. It's a constant search for perfection, fueled by creativity and passion. It's about finding balance in the chaos of the kitchen, and transforming simple ingredients into incredible culinary masterpieces. Therefore, let's take on the challenge, accept that rhythm, as well as revel in the art of timing that adds the flavor of every dish.

The impact of the seasons and traditions on the timing of food is an interesting aspect of the world of food. It's evidence of the strong connection between food and culture and the immense influence that the rhythms of nature have on the dining experience.

The seasons play a crucial influence on the availability and quality of the ingredients which affects the timeframe for food preparation and menu planning. In spring, bright greens and tender veggies signal the introduction of lighter, vibrant meals as the summer bounty of sweet fruits and succulent vegetables encourages refreshing salads and grilled delicious dishes. As autumn begins to set in the root vegetables and rich greens take center stage, indicating the beginning of a more hearty meals that are comforting and nourishing. Winter is the season of strong flavors, with delicious stews, roasted meats and warming spices that dominate the culinary landscape.

Chefs who are adept at utilizing the bounty of the seasons know how crucial timing is the selection of ingredients. They understand that the best freshness and flavor is only achieved when the ingredients are harvested at the ideal time and then quickly incorporated into meals to preserve their original flavor. If it's determining the time of maturing of tomatoes to make the summer gazpacho, and waiting until the frost's first onset to sweeten roots veggies for the winter soup, understanding the cycle of seasons is crucial to culinary success.

The cultural traditions of the past also have an enormous influence on food timings, influencing not just the food we consume but also the way we eat it. From the relaxed pace of the typical Mediterranean meal to the exact rituals of the Japanese tea ceremony social rules dictate the time of rituals and meals according to the beliefs and practices of a particular society. In diverse societies, meals aren't only about eating These are social occasions that bring a chance to connect and celebrate. The time of these events is usually marked by traditions, with meals scheduled around religious festivals, seasonal celebrations, occasions, or milestones in the family. In Italy For instance the time of meals is governed by a strict schedule and lunch is usually served at the beginning of the afternoon and dinner being served late in the night, giving ample time for a leisurely conversations and socializing.

The time of certain food rituals, like the afternoon tea tradition during afternoon tea in England as well as the Japanese custom of kaiseki dining, has a the significance of culture. The rituals are usually based on an ordered sequence of meals and are serving at a particular time and with the customs and practices. It doesn't matter if it's the exact timing of the tea's steeping, or the meticulous pace of a multi-course Kaiseki dinner, these culinary rituals are a way to express the cultural identity and heritage of the region.

Alongside meal times the cultural context also influences the preparation of food and preservation methods. The slow fermenting of Kimchi from Korea to the lengthy slow cooking of the cassoulet in France traditional ways of cooking and preservation of food are typically determined by the cycles of the seasons and availability of the ingredients. These traditional methods will not only boost the flavor and texture of food, but can also be a bridge to the past and connect us to the food practices of our forefathers.

The influence of the seasons and the cultural tradition on food timing is evident. From the choice of ingredients to the time of meals and the rituals that accompany them they influence how we perceive food and infuse our eating experiences with meaning and importance. Through understanding and embracing the rhythms of the natural world and cultural Chefs can create memorable dining experiences that resonate with guests at a deep scale.

When we look into the intricacies of cooking timing it becomes apparent that every moment is a possibility of a culinary breakthrough. Each time a dish is cooked and each ingredient chosen there is a chance to explore new levels of texture, flavor, and smell. It is in these instances that the essence of culinary art reveals its delicate balance of accuracy and intuition, aided by the timing of the food.

In the realm of cooking timing isn't just an operational consideration, but is a crucial component of the creative process. From the meticulous observation of temperatures for cooking to the exact timing of ingredients' additions, every choice taken within the kitchen can be influenced by passing of time. Through this meticulous control of timing that chefs are able get the most full taste out of their food ingredients and transform the ordinary into something truly extraordinary.

The timing of the addition of ingredients can have a significant impact on the final result of the dish. For instance the inclusion of fresh herbs in an sauce. When they wait until the last minutes of cooking to add herbs like cilantro or basil chefs can retain their vibrant color and delicate taste, resulting in a dish not just visually stunning, but also packed with freshness. In contrast adding herbs too soon in the cooking process may make them spongy and dull, depriving your dish freshness.

Alongside the culinary aspects that require precision, time is a key factor in determining our impression of food. Take the excitement that builds when aromas emanate from the kitchen, signalling the food is ready to be taken in. The moment of excitement prior to taking the first bite of an exquisitely cooked steak in which the steak is most tender and delicious. These anticipation-inducing moments that are heightened by the realization that the ideal meal is just a few minutes away, add a new level of pleasure to your dining experience.

The pleasure of each moment during the culinary experience is more than having a great meal. It's about experiencing the wonder of timing that turns ordinary food into something extraordinary. It's about understanding the splendor and depth of the cooking procedure, from the precise selection of ingredients to the exact execution of cooking techniques. It is about enjoying every moment, knowing that there is the possibility of food discovery and enjoyment.

Timing goes beyond the boundaries of the kitchen's busy environment and into the nitty-gritty in the selection of ingredients. In this complex art of cooking fresh ingredients are not just desired, they are vital. Chefs must strike an intricate balance between scheduling their menus to coincide with most popular seasons for diverse ingredients and making sure these ingredients are used in their peak in terms of flavor and freshness.

Take a look at the subtle interplay of flavors in a classic spring tomato salad. To complete perfect culinary quality tomatoes should be cautiously selected at the peak of their ripeness. They're filled with vibrant hues and a heavenly sweet scent. However, this brief time of perfection is fleeting when tomatoes change from overripe to ripe in just a blink. So, timing is the key to ensuring that every ingredient is used to the fullest extent to capture what the seasons offer in each delicious bite.

The world of ingredient choice encompasses an array of tastes of textures, aromas, and textures that each have their distinct seasonal characteristics. From tender, crisp asparagus in spring, to the succulent, sun-ripened pears at the peak of summer The landscape of food is filled with a dazzling assortment of fresh ingredients, each requiring care and attention to detail.

In the field of seafood timing plays a vital role in ensuring the best freshness and taste. For instance that delicate shell of scallops should be procured and used at a precise time to ensure the delicate sweetness and suppleness. Also, the time of the harvest is essential when it comes to selecting oysters, with their taste changing as a result of fluctuations in salinity and temperature of the water. When they master the art of choosing ingredients cooks can transform their meals from being mere food items to truly food experiences, and capture the essence of the ocean in each delicious bite.

It is crucial to consider timing ingredient selection goes beyond freshness. It also involves concerns about sustainability and ethical source. In a time of an increasing awareness of the importance of conservation and animal health, chefs are more conscious of the source of their ingredients as well as the consequences of their culinary choices. By aligning their menus with seasonal availability and ethical methods of sourcing, chefs are able to not only prepare dishes with exceptional quality and taste, but also aid in the conservation of our precious natural resources.

The art of choosing the excellent ingredients can be seen as a proof of the profound link between food and culture each ingredient bringing its own intricate story of tradition, history and significance in the culinary world. From the fragrant spices from India to the rich Italian flavors that are found along the Mediterranean coast The ingredients used by chefs are infused with the tales of generations of the past, creating a vivid story of the culinary history and culture.

The art of selecting the right ingredients is a complex process that goes beyond simply freshness. It's a concert of textures, flavors, and scents that are coordinated with accuracy and precision. By embracing the bounty of the seasons of nature, respecting the ethics of sustainable as well as ethically sourced products, as well as paying tribute to the rich variety of culinary traditions that form the basis of our global culinary landscape, chefs can take their food to new levels in culinary experience. When you get into your kitchen, keep in mind that timing is crucial in the selection of ingredients. It could be the way to unlock a new universe that is full of possibilities for food.

In the bustling kitchen in which the clanging of pans mixes with the smoky aroma of food and the sound of conversation it is the time to be precise. In the midst of confusion and apprehension it is important to recognize that timing isn't always a perfect science. External factors like variations in ingredient quality, variations in the performance of equipment, and even the unpredictable whimsy of the weather could conspire to disrupt the meticulously planned process of creating a culinary masterpiece. Chefs in such situations need to show flexibility, the ability to pivot, adjust and invent to meet unexpected situations. It isn't just an essential survival skill, it's a hallmark of a true artist in the kitchen who is able to turn challenges into opportunities and turning culinary mistakes into moments of awe.

It's not just about responding to the challenges that arise, it's as much about anticipating and making preparations for the possibility of them. Professional chefs are aware that every day in the kitchen are the same. As therefore, they approach each shift with a sense that is flexible and resourceful. They have a fully-stocked pantry prepared to experiment and alter ingredients as required. They have good relationships with suppliers, allowing them to rapidly source substitutes for any ingredient that aren't available. They invest in flexible equipment and refined techniques that enable them to adjust to a variety of food preparation situations with ease and precision.

The ability to adapt extends beyond the kitchen to the wider scope of menu design and development. In today's fast-changing food and beverage industry, chefs have to continuously adapt to changing consumer preferences, new food trends and technological advances. They need to be prepared to try innovative ingredients, techniques and combinations of flavors and push the boundaries of conventional culinary practices to develop dishes that are innovative appealing, interesting, and relevant to modern food preferences. The ability to adapt is what fuels food innovation, driving the growth of gastronomy, and ensuring its continual significance and viability in an ever-changing world.

It's also a mental state approach to challenges that is characterized by the ability to overcome obstacles, with creativity and optimism. It's about accepting the unexpected and turning setbacks into possibilities, refusing be discouraged by the challenges. When it comes to cooking, and in all aspects of life, those who can adapt can thrive when faced with the unknown, finding an inspiration in any obstacle, and becoming healthier and stronger.

The ability to adapt is the foundation of success in the world of food and drink. It is a essential skill that allows cooks to maneuver the constantly changing culinary landscape with grace and ingenuity. With a focus on agility as well as resourcefulness and resilience Chefs can conquer any obstacle, turning mistakes to moments of brilliance transform the mundane into the extraordinary. So next time you're cooking, think about the importance of flexibility. It could be the ingredient that will take the quality of your food to higher levels of excellence.

Timing is essential in ingredient preparation and synchronization. If you are chopping vegetables or marinating meats, the process must be meticulously timed to ensure that all ingredients work seamlessly in the final meal. It is vital to ensure the efficiency of the process and that all the components of a dish are ready to serve simultaneously.

Timing is a factor in the development of flavor and the complexity of cooking. Slow cooking techniques such as braising can increase the taste of dishes by allowing ingredients to mix in time. Also, the timing of herbs and spices will significantly affect the intensity and depth of the flavor profile, with every ingredient contributing its distinctive flavor precisely at the right time.

The perfect texture and mouthfeel are dependent on the precise timing. Whether you want a crisp crust layer over a seared steak or to ensure creamy consistency in a risotto d doesn't matterish. Timing is a crucial factor. The wrong cooking technique or ingredients can cause unpleasant textures, reducing the overall taste of the meal.

Timing is essential to maintain temperature control and the integrity of the ingredients. Ensuring proteins are cooked to the proper internal temperature will ensure food safety and a perfect texture. Additionally, adjusting the cooking process to avoid overexposure to heat will keep components from drying and losing moisture, thus preserving their quality and taste.

The Other Five Senses

Cooking timing is intertwined with seasonal and cultural considerations. Many cuisines have traditional recipes and are prepared at specific dates of the year, usually to coincide with seasonal ingredients or celebrations. Respecting these customs and understanding the seasonal availability of ingredients is crucial to achieving the most efficient cooking timing.

Chefs should be able to adapt and be adept at problem-solving. If unexpected issues occur, such as food ingredient shortages or equipment malfunctions, Chefs must alter their cooking techniques and timing to overcome challenges and warrant a successful dish.

The last few minutes before serving a meal are crucial for the presentation and plating. It is essential to warrant that each element is carefully and with diligence, which increases the appearance of a dish and entices guests before they take the first bite.

Timing is not limited to cooking and can include finishing and resting methods. Letting cooked meats rest before cutting will ensure that juices distribute evenly, leading to the most moist and delicious end product. The finishing process should be scheduled just before serving to maintain the flavor and vibrancy.

Timing is essential to balance an item's sweet and sour, salty or bitter taste. The exact timing of ingredients and cooking procedures is crucial to blending these flavor elements and providing a balanced food experience.

When it comes to aging, timing becomes a valuable ally that directs the maturing process toward the best possible development of flavor. To produce cheeses of unmatched complexity, cheesemakers carefully monitor aging chambers, regulating temperature and humidity to promote the slow breakdown of proteins and lipids. In a same vein, winemakers carefully control how long wines age by adjusting temperature and air exposure to extract complex flavors and velvety tannins. The secret to expertise is not only knowing when to step in, but also letting time do its alchemical magic and turn uncooked components into delicious treats.

Timing is a mutually beneficial relationship between fermentation and aging, despite their different approaches. In both cases, the passage of time is the driving force behind the development of flavor, and the right timing is the hand that guides the process in the direction of culinary perfection. Think about the craft of beer making, where age and fermentation combine to produce a harmonious blend of flavors. Brewers skillfully coordinate every step of the process, using timing to produce the ideal balance of bitterness, sweetness, and complexity in anything from hop-forward ales to barrel-aged stouts.

The practice of fermentation and aging is fundamentally an expression of a deep reverence for time and its capacity for transformation. Whether making aged wines, sourdough loaves, or artisanal cheeses, artisans are aware of the fine balance between taste and timing. They unravel the mysteries of fermentation and aging with perseverance, practice, and a profound understanding of microbial alchemy, bringing a plethora of delectable culinary treats to the globe.

When it comes to culinary alchemy, timing is everything. It's the silent mastermind behind flavor metamorphosis. When components are used at the right moment, they become more than just ingredients and become culinary marvels. This is evident in everything from the seething cauldrons of fermenting dough to the peaceful caves housing aged cheeses. Let us keep in mind the age-old lesson that time, when handled with skill and care, has the ability to transform common foods and beverages into unique sensory experiences as we continue to delve into the mysteries of fermentation and aging.

When cooking sous vide, the timing is carefully controlled to produce the exact outcome. Ingredients are vacuum sealed and cooked in a precisely controlled water bath for prolonged durations, allowing flavors to be evenly infused and the textures to soften.

Timing is vital for emulsification and thickening procedures, such as making dressings and sauces. Making additions of ingredients such as eggs or oil gradually and at the correct temperature ensures the proper emulsification that results in a uniform and stable mix. Also, ensuring that you add thickeners such as cornstarch or flour on time will ensure that sauces attain the desired consistency without getting too thick or lumpy.

Simmering and reduction techniques depend on precise timing to concentrate flavors and produce delicious stock and sauces. Slow simmering lets ingredients release flavors slowly while reducing the liquid by evaporation, which enhances flavors and makes sauces thicker. The timing is essential for these processes to stop sauces from being reduced too much or too concentrated, resulting in a delicious and balanced final product.

On the opposite side of the coin timing also influences the degrading of food nutrients while cooking. The overcooking process or the prolonged exposure to heat may cause the loss of minerals, vitamins, and other vital nutrients. Learning the proper cooking timings and cooking techniques can help keep the nutritional value of food items.

The timing is crucial for seasoning and tasting food during preparation. Adding salt, herbs, and spices at the perfect time allows flavors to blend and intensify, increasing the overall flavor of the food. Continuous testing throughout cooking assures that changes can be made to complete the ideal balance of seasoning and balance.

The timing for garnishing and completing the look is vital to increasing dishes' aesthetic appeal and richness. Fresh condiments, herbs, and garnishes should be added shortly before serving to ensure their freshness and vibrant flavor, improving the appearance and overall dining experience.

In the complex cooking process, timing is the primary factor influencing each culinary aspect. From precise preparation techniques to accurate synchronization of ingredients, timing can affect the taste and texture, presentation, and overall dining experience. Through mastering this art, they can unlock the possibilities of their ingredients, turning ordinary ingredients into extraordinary food creations that excite all the senses while feeding the body and soul. So, the next time you are in the kitchen, be aware of the significance of timing. It could be the solution to unlocking the new world in culinary options.

In the harmonious blend of flavors that chefs craft, time assumes the role of the maestro, coordinating every component to craft the epitome of culinary excellence. A keen sense of timing distinguishes amateurs from experts in the kitchen, guiding the fusion of ingredients, adjustments in temperature, and the precise moment to complete a dish. Cultivating this timing prowess is essential for crafting flawlessly cooked meals brimming with diverse textures and rich flavors. This comprehensive guide will explore effective strategies for honing your timing skills in the kitchen, spanning from mastering ingredient cooking durations to optimizing multitasking capabilities.

Mastering timing is integral to maximizing the potential of cooking, particularly in understanding the varying cooking durations of diverse ingredients. Each ingredient possesses distinct attributes such as texture, density, and flavor profile, influencing the required cooking duration for optimal results. While robust root vegetables and tough meats necessitate prolonged cooking to tenderize and develop flavor, delicate seafood and greens demand swift and precise cooking to prevent overcooking. With proficiency in ingredient-specific cooking times and adeptness in adapting cooking techniques accordingly, one can elevate culinary prowess and craft dishes distinguished by impeccable timing and flavor.

In the culinary arts, mastering the art of timing cooking times for ingredients is crucial. It's the base where delicious and well-cooked meals are constructed. Each component has a distinctive characteristic, which requires a particular focus on timing to achieve the best payoff. Root vegetables like carrots and potatoes and tough cuts of beef require longer cooking times to remove their fibrous textures and to develop a rich taste. In contrast, delicate seafood and greens require quick cooking to preserve soft textures and delicate flavors.

When chefs know the cooking time of various ingredients, they can prepare the cooking procedures precisely. This allows for adequate meal preparation and ensures that all the components of a dish are prepared to serve at the same time. This also helps prevent the overcooked or undercooked components from being cooked, creating a balanced blend of flavors and textures for the final product.

Additionally, the choice of cooking technique is essential in determining the cooking duration. A stew or braising method is ideal for meats with tougher cuts because the lengthy, slow cooking process allows collagen to disintegrate, creating succulent and tender food items. On the other hand, fast-cooking techniques like stir-frying and sauteing are best suited to succulent meat and vegetables since they cook quickly over high temperatures while retaining their moisture and flavor.

Incorporating different cooking techniques in meal preparation helps chefs streamline their cooking procedures and ensure that everything cooks promptly. When they choose the best method for every ingredient, be it grilling, braising, or roasting. Chefs will be able to complete the same delicious and consistent payoff effortlessly. Ultimately, they had a sense of timing when cooking, which is crucial to creating dishes that are not just tasty but visually appealing and balanced. By knowing the various cooking times for different ingredients and using cooking techniques carefully, chefs can enhance their food knowledge and delight guests with delicious meals cooked perfectly every time.

In culinary understanding, the art of blending cooking methods is vital for transforming dishes from simple meals into refined culinary masterpieces. Apart from mastering ingredient cooking times, incorporating diverse cooking techniques is essential for creating a cohesive culinary experience. It's akin to conducting an ensemble where each cooking technique contributes to a unified blend of flavors, aromas, textures, and sensations.

The Other Five Senses

In the exciting world of the culinary field, where skill is paired with passion, understanding the fine art of timing goes far beyond simple calculations and watch-keeping. While knowing the cooking times of ingredients and synchronizing cooking techniques are essential pillars of the craft, there is another aspect–an area of intuition that sets experienced chefs apart. The ability to sense timing or the sixth sense developed through training, observation, practice, and a solid connection to the craft of cooking can make the standard of a dish outstanding.

When you begin your culinary adventure, accept that the ability to discern is as important an instrument as any spatula or knife you have. The whisper guides your hands when it stirs, turns, or adds seasoning, leading you to the perfect culinary experience with every graceful movement.

The ability to discern timing is developed through experience, refined through countless hours at the table, and then refined by an experiment of trial and trial. Each time you cook, you become aware of the subtle signals that tell you the ingredients are ready to transform into delicious dishes. It doesn't matter if it's the sound of onions simmering in the hot pan or the scent of freshly baked bread floating across your air. These signals are your compass that will guide you to the highest food quality.

Pay attention to the sensory and visual cues while you cook. Please pay attention to how the color of your vegetables changes as they cook, transforming from bright and raw to soft and caramelized. Be aware of the resistance in the meat while it cooks, and gauge its cooked enough with the gentle pressure of your fingers. Inhale deeply as the aromas mix and change into a complex blend of flavors waiting to be enjoyed.

As you improve your innate timing, remember that repetition is the key to becoming perfect. Take every opportunity to experiment and grow, accepting the setbacks and successes as you go. Every time you create a new dish, your sense of taste and intuition will strengthen, helping you achieve ever-greater culinary achievements. Making the right decisions about timing isn't solely about cooking. It's about creating an intimate connection to the food you cook and the pleasure it gives to the people who eat at your table. Therefore, trust your intuition, enjoy the adventure, and let your gut guide you as you begin your culinary journey.

Knowing the subtleties of temperature and heat is vital to mastering an acute sense of timing while cooking. From the tiniest simmer of a stew to the blazing heat of a grill, heat manipulation transforms ingredients into tasty food items. By learning how heat interacts with food items and mastering the art of temperature control, cooks can be energetic about how their food ends energetically. Every ingredient is at its maximum at the pond.

The process of heat transfer consists of energy being transferred from a source of heat to the food that is being cooked. It is essential to know the different methods of heat transfer, including conduction, convection, and radiation. Conduction is a direct heat transfer method, like grilling an entrée in a hot pan. Convection is circulating hot liquid or air around the food item, typically in baking or roasting. Radiation radiates heat from an absorbed source into the food, such as when grilling or broiling.

The precise control of temperature is crucial for consistently cooking payoff. When together, stovetops or ovens, grills, or any other appliance that can alter and maintain the desired temperature will ensure uniform cooking and levels of doneness. The precision of temperature control allows chefs to complete certain degrees of doneness, namely medium, rare, or well-done for the meats, or even al soft, al dente, or the caramelization of vegetables.

The Maillard reaction happens as a chemical reaction between sugars and amino acids when they are heated, which causes color change and the development of flavor. Understanding how heat triggers Maillard's response is crucial to developing depth of taste in dishes like seared steaks, roasted veggies, and baked goods. By controlling the temperature and cooking time, chefs can control their Maillard reactions to fulfill the desired amounts of caramelization for example and enhance flavor.

Protein denaturation refers to the change in proteins when exposed to heat, which affects the texture and consistency. Understanding how heat affects protein denaturation is vital to getting the desired textures from seafood, meats, poultry, and eggs. The tenderness of a seared steak, the flakiness of grilled fish, the creamy taste of poached eggs, and the exact temperature control will warrant that protein is cooked to perfection.

The heat also causes the ingredients' moisture to disappear, affecting the cooking time and the texture. Understanding the impact of heat on the loss of moisture is vital to ensuring no dryness or hardness in cooked meals. For instance, slow-cooking techniques such as stewing or braising allow the collagen's breakdown while keeping moisture, leading to succulent and soft meats.

Every cooking oil has a particular smoking point, the temperature at which it begins breaking down to generate smoke. Knowing the smoke points of various oils is vital to preserving flavor and avoiding bitter or burned taste in foods. Using oils with higher smoke points when using high-temperature cooking techniques like searing or frying helps maintain the integrity of the ingredients and their flavors.

The type of cookware you use can affect the distribution of heat and cook efficiency. Materials such as cast iron or copper are highly heat-conductive and distribute heat evenly across the cooking surface, permitting accurate temperature regulation. Understanding the characteristics of different cookware materials can help chefs choose the most appropriate vessels to cook with various techniques and food items.

The time between cooking and resting allows the heat to be distributed throughout the food, ensuring uniform cooking and improving the flavor. Knowing the notion of carryover cooking - where food cooks for a long time after it has been removed from the source of heat - helps avoid overcooking and ensures that dishes are served at the highest quality. To master the fundamentals of temperature and heat, chefs can collect cooking timing knowledge and create perfectly delicious, tasty, and memorable dishes.

Cooking is a form of art that requires a delicate blend of talent, creativity, and timing. From searing a steak until perfect perfection to simmering sauce until it is at an ideal consistency, each step of the cooking process requires exact timing. But can timing become an automatic process after years of working cooking? Do experienced cooks intuitively know when their food is done without using recipes or timers? This is a question I get asked a lot.

When you're starting to cook, the timing of your food can seem overwhelming. You might find yourself looking up recipe ideas, setting times, and frantically checking the food you cook to ensure they do not overcook or overheat it. As you receive experience cooking, you'll begin to gain knowledge of how the ingredients behave and how heat impacts them. This understanding is developed by observation, practice, and trial.

Repetition is the key to developing an intuitive sense of timing when cooking. The more time you spend cooking one dish and getting more experienced, the more acquainted you get with its subtleties and the time required to obtain what you want outcome. With time, the more you cook, obtain faith in your skills and rely less on external indicators like timers or recipes. Instead, you are taught to trust your intuition and rely on your senses, like smell, sight, and touch, to judge a dish's perfection level.

Knowing how different ingredients react when heated is crucial to gaining the ability to sense timing when cooking. For instance, proteins like poultry and meat experience modifications in their texture as well as color when they cook, whereas vegetables become soft and release their natural juices. If you're familiar with the properties of different ingredients, you can predict how they react to various cooking techniques and alter your cooking time accordingly.

Mastering various cooking methods is another part of acquiring an intuitive sense of timing. Every technique needs precise timing to fulfill the most optimal outcome when it comes to sautéing, roasting, braising, or grilling. As you learn these techniques and become adept at their execution, you'll understand the timing signals of every method.

Experienced cooks also can adapt to various cooking conditions and kitchen equipment. When cooking on a gas range or electric range and an outside grill. Each configuration has its own set of difficulties and requires adjustments to timing. Through experience, you'll learn how to deal with these variations and adjust your cooking methods to ensure the same payoff regardless of the situation.

The inevitable mistakes are an element of learning when cooking. However, they can also teach invaluable lessons on timing. When you fail to cook a steak or a batch of cookies or over-season the sauce, every mistake can be a chance to consider your mistakes and ways you can rise the next time. In time, you'll make mistakes that you can learn from and better understand the timing involved in cooking.

Ultimately, getting a natural understanding of cooking timing is all about developing your culinary intuition. It's about listening to your senses, relying on your intuition, and enjoying playing around when cooking. While external cues like timers or recipes can be helpful, true mastery is found in the inherent knowledge from decades of expertise and a love for cooking.

Although timing might not be effortless, it gets more natural with time. Experienced cooks develop confidence in their intuitions, trust their senses, and adapt to various cooking environments. Through observation, practice, and the ability to learn from mistakes, they develop a natural understanding of timing, which lets them repeatedly create delicious and exquisitely executed dishes.

The culinary adventure to master the art of cooking isn't all about adhering to recipes strictly, it's about taking risks and making mistakes that happen in the process. It's a trip of exciting discoveries, unforeseen flavors, and, sometimes, a mishap. However, don't worry

The Other Five Senses

about it because every mistake is a chance to improve your skills, boost your knowledge, and eventually, become an improved cook.

The first and most important thing is not to be afraid to fail. Hinder you from trying new methods, ingredients, and flavor profiles. In the kitchen, you are your place to play; experimentation is how to unleash your culinary imagination. If it's trying a new recipe you've not tried before or playing around with the ingredients at your kitchen counter, enjoy the excitement of exploring the culinary world with an open mind.

Don't get discouraged when you make mistakes, and they will happen. Instead, see these as learning opportunities, eventually making you an even better cook. Did your souffle fall apart during baking? Did the sauce break, or did your bread appear denser than anticipated? Consider a moment to reflect on what went wrong and, most importantly, why. Was it a problem with the temperature timing or even the method used? Once you have identified the issue's root, you will know an excellent way to avoid similar problems in the future.

Don't undervalue the power of reflection and observation during learning. Be aware of the subtle aspects of cooking - how ingredients react with heat, how flavors evolve as time passes, and how flavors change as you progress through your cooking. Suppose you sharpen your observational skills and observe your cooking. In that case, you'll comprehend the intricacies of timing when cooking and become more proficient in anticipating and adapting to the requirements of your meals.

Alongside hands-on experiences, look for sources that can increase your culinary abilities and sharpen your knowledge. Cookbooks, cooking classes, and online tutorials are excellent methods for learning new techniques, experimenting with various cuisines, and getting insights from experienced chefs. Don't be afraid to ask questions, play with new recipes, and get ideas from many sources. The more you get immersed in cooking, the more comfortable and skilled you'll be in making your meals perfect.

Ultimately, getting the ability to judge timing in cooking is a learning and development path. It's an adventure that is filled with victories as well as setbacks, successes, and failures. Be open to the process, be proud of your achievements, and learn by observing your failures. Every time you try a new culinary endeavor, you'll receive more appreciation for the science and art of cooking. Additionally, your knowledge remains to grow and rise with time.

Don't be intimidated to get your hands dirty. Be adventurous, try new things, and test the limits of your comfort zone in the kitchen. Making mistakes and learning from them is vital to mastering timing when cooking. Therefore, take the time to embrace the journey, relish the flavor, and let your curiosity about food lead you on the exciting journey of becoming a better cook.

It's a delicate process of flavors, textures, and timing. Even the tiniest change in the ingredients, cooking methods, or environmental conditions could significantly affect how food is cooked. While figuring out the excellent cooking times for ingredients and synchronizing cooking techniques are essential aspects of culinary proficiency, It is crucial to realize that other variables are critical in the cooking process. From the properties of the ingredients themselves to the equipment utilized and the conditions within which cooking occurs, These variables have the power to profoundly impact the final result of the dish. When they are aware of and consider these elements, chefs can modify and improve their cooking methods and warrant consistent, delicious payoffs for each cooking endeavor.

The quality of the ingredients is the main factor that affects the cooking time. Factors like dimensions, shape, density, content, and ripeness contribute to how fast or slow the ingredients cook. For instance, smaller and thinner pieces of beef or other vegetables will generally cook faster than thicker or larger pieces. Additionally, food items with a high moisture content, like freshly cut tomatoes and mushrooms, could require longer cooking times to evaporate liquid and concentrate flavors.

The temperature at which ingredients start cooking will also affect cooking time. Ingredients at room temperature cook faster and more evenly than cold ingredients from the fridge. For instance, allowing the meat to cool to room temperature before cooking will ensure the most uniform cooking and prevent cooking from overheating on the outside while the interior remains undercooked. Similarly, using room-temperature ingredients in baking can result in an excellent texture and a higher rise in baked products.

The cooking method and equipment used will significantly impact the time spent cooking. Different methods, including braising, grilling, or steaming, apply heat to the ingredients in various ways, which results in other times and results. In addition, the design and performance of the cooking apparatus, like electric and gas stoves, conventional or convection ovens, or cooking equipment that is of high quality or low quality, will affect how fast or evenly the ingredients cook.

The altitude of the area and the environmental conditions, like humidity and ambient temperature, also affect cooking duration. At higher elevations, where air pressure is lower, water boils slower and at a lower temperature, affecting the cooking times of various ingredients like pasta and grains. Additionally, high humidity can delay evaporation and extend cooking times. On the other hand, low humidity can speed up the process of evaporation and decrease cooking time. The temperature of the air can influence the efficiency of cooking equipment, as well as the speed at which food items cook.

Recipes can be modified, such as substituting or adding ingredients, or omissions can affect the cooking time. For instance, canned beans instead of dried beans in a recipe could cut down on cooking time since canned beans have already been softened and cooked. Additionally, adding other ingredients with a higher moisture content, such as fruits or vegetables, could boost cooking time by adding more liquids to the dish.

Resting time and cooking for carryover are crucial aspects to consider, mainly when cooking baked goods and meat. The time that meat is allowed to rest before cutting allows the juices to distribute and flavors to blend, resulting in more juicy and softer meat. In addition, carryover cooking – the continued cooking of food even after it's removed from the source of heat can alter the final cooking time of the dish. For instance, a steak will continue cooking in its resting state, and removing it from the source of heat a little before reaching the desired degree of doneness will prevent it from overcooking.

Individual preferences and dietary restrictions can also affect cooking times. Certain people may prefer vegetables cooked until they have a crisp and tender texture, whereas others like them to be softer. Also, specific dietary restrictions that include gluten-free, vegan, vegetarian, or low-sodium diets might require modifications to cooking techniques and ingredients and cooking time to accommodate specific food preferences or dietary requirements.

While understanding cook times for ingredients and synchronizing cooking techniques are crucial elements of culinary proficiency, It's essential to identify and consider the many other factors that impact the cooking process. Through analyzing factors like the nature of the ingredient, its characteristics, the temperature at which it starts as well as cooking methods and equipment as well as altitude and environmental conditions, recipes with variations as well as resting times, carryover cooking as well as the individual's preferences and dietary restrictions, Chefs can adjust and improve their method of cooking, and warrant consistent, delicious outcome every time they cook.

Time is undoubtedly an essential element of culinary science. It is interspersed throughout every step of cooking. From the exact timing of ingredients to the length of cooking methods, time plays an essential role in determining the final result of the final product. This is why understanding the concept of time is crucial for any budding kitchen chef and home cook.

In culinary science, time isn't just several minutes, seconds, or hours but an active force that affects chemicals, flavor development, and texture transformation. Consider, for instance, the process of caramelization, which is the conversion of sugars to complex sweet and nutty tastes by using temperatures over time. When you are sautéing onions or grilling meats, the time spent cooking directly affects the amount of caramelization achieved, eventually impacting your dish's taste and appearance.

Timing is a crucial factor in the execution of cooking methods. From braising and simmering to baking and roasting, every technique must be executed carefully to ensure that all ingredients are cooked perfectly. For sample, a few minutes could mean an essential difference between a soft and tender roast and one that's too dry or overcooked. In the same way, how much time you adjust the temperature in the emulsification process, such as making mayonnaise or hollandaise sauce – can determine the consistency and stability of the end product.

Time is an essential factor in the preservation and safety of food. The correct cooking time is necessary to eliminate harmful pathogens and bacteria that could be present in raw food ingredients. In addition, processes like curing, fermentation, and aging depend on controlled periods to alter ingredients and create distinct flavors. For instance, the duration of fermentation affects the tang of sourdough, and the aging process adds the richness of flavor to the cured cheeses and meats.

It's an essential factor in the kitchen and a vital food science principle. It helps transform the raw ingredients into delicious dishes, controls the success of cooking methods, and ensures food quality and safety. So, knowing how to master timing is crucial to achieving the highest culinary proficiency and creating an unforgettable dining experience, and through practice, observation, or even a thorough understanding of science, accepting the importance of time when cooking is a sign that a chef is skilled.

CHAPTER FIVE

A Sense of D.F.C
(Discipline, Focus & Consistency)

The culinary industry isn't only about ingredients and recipes. It's a form of art that requires thorough knowledge of the importance of focus, discipline, and consistency. These three components aren't only qualities but the foundation of a successful culinary experience. These three elements transform the cooking process from a straightforward job into an artistic expression and a lucrative career. Culinary discipline requires adhering to recipes, techniques, and standards. Focus will allow you to focus on completing the task flawlessly and consistently. This ensures that every dish meets the standards the chef or restaurant sets each time.

The influence of discipline, focus, and consistency (D.F.C) on culinary and establishment careers can't be overstated. These principles play an essential role in the culinary industry, affecting everything from the individual development of a chef's experience to food-related companies' overall achievement. The path of a chef or the development of a food establishment is deeply influenced by the degree to which these concepts are understood, accepted, and utilized.

Beginning with discipline, it's the foundation of success in cooking. In a kitchen, discipline is more than the simple process of following recipes and following the time of service. It is the commitment to ongoing improvement and learning, the care and attention to detail in choosing ingredients, and the constant striving for perfection in every job, whether it's the preparation of a basic broth or a sophisticated multi-course meal. Chefs who have this discipline can translate it into an organized approach to their work, meaning each step in the kitchen is deliberate, and every aspect is considered. This approach to discipline does not just enhance your talent and knowledge but prepares you for the pressures and challenges of the fast-paced food industry. For establishments in the culinary industry employees, a disciplined workforce assures the consistency of the quality of food, efficiency in operations, and adherence to safety and health standards and regulations, all of which are essential to the success of the establishment and its sustainability.

In the culinary arts field, the foundation upon which the whole profession is built is the culinary arts discipline. It's a broad concept that applies to all aspects of cooking, from the beginning stages of a chef's training to the day-to-day activities of the world's most highly regarded kitchens. This extensive study explores the different levels of discipline required in the kitchen and demonstrates its importance for achieving quality food.

The journey to the world of food begins with training and education, where discipline is made a prerequisite. Culinary education isn't just about learning how to cook. It's about knowing the scientific basis behind cooking techniques, culinary art history, and diet's significance. It requires a disciplined approach to learning through hands-on training and constant learning. Students must follow strict schedules, organize their time well between the theoretical and practical classes, and devote their time to learning the fundamentals before moving on to more complex tasks. The culinary discipline taught in culinary schools sets the foundation for subsequent endeavors in the kitchen.

The discipline extends to carefully choosing food ingredients, which requires patience, knowledge, and dedication to high quality. Chefs need to choose ingredients that do not just enhance the flavor of their food but also meet their ethics and health standards. This requires establishing connections with suppliers, recognizing the seasons of produce, and going to farms and markets to warrant the high quality of the ingredients. A disciplined chef recognizes how the caliber of ingredients directly impacts the result of the dish and, thus, is not compromising on this essential component of the cooking process.

The most important aspect of discipline is respect for hygiene and food safety standards. This element of discipline is crucial to ensure the safety and health of patrons, preventing their health from foodborne illnesses and providing an enjoyable dining experience. Professionals in the kitchen and chefs must adhere to strict guidelines when storing, preparing, and serving food, such as maintaining appropriate temperatures, avoiding cross-contamination, and keeping the kitchen clean. This type of discipline requires ongoing vigilance and dedication to perfect practices in every step undertaken within the kitchen.

Discipline in food is also a commitment to mastering the art of cooking. It requires an early morning start, long work hours, and the constant pursuit of perfection. Chefs have to be able to practice their talent often, test new methods, and be open to improvement and learning. This commitment is what transforms the most straightforward dinner into a culinary masterpiece. It's about taking that step to warrant that each plate served out of the kitchen reflects the chef's dedication to their craft.

It is a highly complicated and sometimes chaotic space that requires discipline to ensure success. Chefs must manage many tasks simultaneously, including preparing ingredients and coordinating every dish element precisely. This requires efficiency, planning, and focus, which can only be achieved with discipline. Chefs must also collaborate with their staff, communicating energetically and ensuring everyone is in sync when delivering extraordinary culinary experiences to their guests.

For those who want to become chefs, discipline is the driving force that guides them from beginning to mastery of their trade. They can develop their skills, build their reputations, and advance their careers through discipline. The culinary industry is highly competitive, and only those committed to their profession can hope to make a mark. The discipline of chefs allows them to go beyond their limitations to be innovative and creative and to help develop the culinary field.

Discipline is the basis on which excellence in culinary is built. It is a guiding principle in every aspect of the cooking profession, including the selection of ingredients, education on food safety, and perfecting one's skills. A disciplined chef values their craft, their clients, and the rich tradition of the world of food. They recognize that discipline isn't a restriction but an empowering force that allows chefs to be creative, invent, and complete top-quality standards for culinary perfection. Discipline is the only way to ensure culinary pursuits will continue to enthrall, delight, and unite people in the spirit of good food.

The notion of discipline, especially in the culinary arts, goes beyond the traditional limits of compliance or control. The kitchen is where discipline is the foundation that holds up the creative chaos and ensures that the culinary creations are replicated with the same enthusiasm and accuracy as the chef intended. This in-depth look at the role of discipline in culinary art will examine its many facets and effect on productivity, creativity, learning, and finally, the culinary experience delivered to diners.

The pillar of precision and consistency in the world of cooking embodies more than simply adherence to clearly defined recipes, procedures, and the high standards set by well-qualified chefs. It signifies a commitment to understanding and mastering the complex science and art that every ingredient and cooking method is a part of. It is not just about a follow-through of the recipe's instructions but requires understanding the reasoning behind each step and the effect of each ingredient in the dish.

Chefs invest a long time perfecting their craft, learning abilities that span from precise techniques for cutting to accurate control of temperatures. The strict instruction and discipline ensure that each dish prepared in the kitchen is prepared to a level of quality. The main goal of this systematic approach is consistency, ensuring that the signature dish has the same flavor, texture, and presentation, whether prepared for an incredibly busy lunchtime or a more secluded dining experience. It is essential to maintain this consistency to prepare patrons with a predictable and reliable dining experience that exceeds the expectations of every time.

In the culinary field, precision isn't only about exact measurements or following a prescribed procedure; it's about knowing that there is harmony and balance in ingredients. A skilled chef is aware that changing the amount of one ingredient can drastically alter the dish's overall flavor. They are mindful of the importance of temperature and timing and know how these variables affect the texture and taste of food items. For instance, the exact temperature at which fish is cooked may be between moist fish fillets and dried, overcooked fish. Also, the precise time when adding herbs to a dish will enhance the flavor, which means they will add flavor to the final dish rather than absorbing or losing their flavor.

The art of maintaining accuracy and consistency extends beyond individual meals to the whole restaurant menu and the dining experience. It is the deliberate decision-making of food ingredients. Chefs frequently take great care to procure the desirable top-quality meats, produce, and other ingredients. This focus on quality ensures that each ingredient is a part of the food as intended while preserving the integrity and final result of the chef's work.

Additionally, this discipline impacts the cleanliness and organization of the kitchen. A clean and organized kitchen with every appliance and ingredient placed in the right place allows chefs to perform their tasks more efficiently and effectively, further supporting the aim of uniformity. Cleanliness also plays a crucial role in this. Cleaning and maintaining a clean kitchen ensures that food items are safe to consume and free of any contamination that can impact the food's taste and security.

The influence of discipline on consistency and precision also extends to the development and training of kitchen personnel. Chefs with experience pass on their skills and talent to apprentices, junior chefs, and even the general public. They stressed that discipline was essential to their kitchen methods. This knowledge transfer ensures that the institution's high standards for food and drink are maintained throughout the kitchen. Every chef knows and applies the principles of consistency and precision when working.

The importance of technology and innovations in maintaining consistency and precision can't be ignored. The food industry has taken on technological advancements, including sous-vide equipment, precision ovens, and digital thermometers, to complete more control over cooking techniques. These tools aid chefs in maintaining precise cooking temperatures and time, which contributes to the consistency of their dishes.

The rigorous pursuit of precision and consistency in the food world indicates the passion and dedication of chefs and professionals in the field. It is a testimony to their commitment to their work, understanding the science and art behind cooking, and delivering customers an outstanding dining experience. This systematic approach ensures that each meal they serve isn't just a short-term satisfaction but an unforgettable experience that represents the culmination of many years of training, knowledge, experience, and an unwavering commitment to excellence in food.

The principle of consistency and precision, backed with discipline and consistency in culinary arts, is the foundation of any dining establishment's identity and success. It's what separates the common from the exceptional, turning ordinary meals into exquisite culinary creations. With discipline, chefs can navigate through the complicated interplay of flavors, techniques, and textures to produce recipes that are both high-quality and exceptional in how they are executed. The constant pursuit of quality and consistency ensures that the culinary arts will continue to grow and push the limits of what can be achieved in food while maintaining the integrity and quality that mark exquisite cuisine.

The culinary arts are an illustrative example of the synergy between creativity and discipline. This may appear paradoxical to some because discipline can conjure images of rigidity and conformity, whereas creativity is typically linked to spontaneity and freedom. In food preparation, discipline is not viewed as a blockade to creativity; instead, it creates an excellent framework that takes culinary imagination to new heights.

The base of every tremendous culinary masterpiece is the ability to master essential knowledge and know-how. This includes everything from the accuracy of knife abilities to understanding the impact of different cooking techniques on ingredients. A chef should know how to cut a piece of fish with a touch of finesse, roast food items to the highest quality, and emulsify sauces with the correct consistency. This talent may seem simple or insignificant to a non-skillful, but they are the foundation of the foundation upon which creativity is constructed. Furthermore, the culinary industry is governed by specific rules and guidelines that warrant that food is delicious and safe to consume. They include knowing the food safety guidelines, nutrition fundamentals, and the science underlying cooking. Once chefs understand these rules and policies, they can experiment and develop as they know the boundaries to conduct their business safely.

A significant and crucial aspect of the culinary arts is the ability to comprehend and manipulate flavor. To create a dish that is well-balanced and pleasing to the senses requires a profound knowledge of how various flavors function together. You don't learn this by chance, but it results from a long period of disciplined learning and training.

The Other Five Senses

Chefs are taught to understand and appreciate all the subtleties within every ingredient and how they can be combined or contrasted to obtain a harmonious meal. This systematic approach to mastering flavor lets the process of creativity blossom. Chefs can think outside of the box, mixing unusual ingredients or unconventional techniques to create fresh and thrilling flavor combinations.

In the same way, texture is a critical element in the overall enjoyment of the dish. The contrast between crunchy and smooth or soft and firm can transform a typical dinner into a memorable experience. To complete the perfect texture, you need exact cooking techniques only achieved by disciplined training. Chefs work for hours to perfect their methods to ensure that every element of their food contributes to the desired texture experience. This method of mastering textures can be an excellent canvas for creative thinking and allows chefs to experiment using a variety of combinations and techniques that will surprise and delight their guests.

The rigors of the well-qualified kitchen might seem to be an inconvenient location for creativity to flourish. However, it is within this framework of discipline that chefs can invent. The limitations of working to the menu, observing costs, and ensuring the same dishes are replicated require chefs to think outside the box. They are taught to make do with their available ingredients, often resulting in unexpected ideas and breakthroughs. The ability to solve problems creatively is the direct result of the disciplined setting in their work environment, showing that limitations can inspire creativity.

Culinary expertise also requires reverence and discipline to understand heritage and tradition. Chefs are educated about the background of their profession by studying the classic recipes and techniques handed down through generations. The knowledge of the history of food should not be seen as a hindrance but as a source of inspiration. By mastering traditional methods, chefs can break boundaries, mixing traditional and contemporary techniques to make dishes that pay tribute to their heritage while providing something completely fresh. This method of keeping with tradition will warrant that the new culinary concepts are rooted in a profound knowledge of the art.

At its heart, culinary education is a blend of science, art, and a strict system of discipline. The discipline goes beyond the boundaries of traditional classroom instruction, encompassing all aspects of a student's path to becoming a skillful chef. It transforms students into professionals who excel and recognize the significance of their roles in the culinary industry.

In the realm of culinary education, the cultivation of discipline starts with the acquisition of foundational skills. From the beginning, students are instructed in knife skills, comprehension of taste characteristics, proficiency in culinary methods ranging from sautéing to sous-vide, and the capacity to execute recipes accurately. This intensive training cultivates in them a profound admiration for the art and the self-control necessary to manage it with exceptional proficiency. The accuracy and care imparted at culinary schools are evident in every chopped vegetable, filleted fish, and plated meal. This degree of specificity guarantees that students not only acquire the skill of cooking but also comprehend the significance of uniformity and excellence in their culinary endeavors.

The Other Five Senses

The concept of discipline within culinary education extends beyond the simple observance of rules or adherence to norms. The focus is on developing a mentality that appreciates accuracy, esteem, endurance, and an unwavering commitment to achieving the highest standards. The principles above are crucial for acquiring culinary expertise and cultivating interpersonal qualities that define an authentic practitioner in the realm of culinary arts. As students go from the classroom to the professional kitchen, the self-control they acquire forms the basis for their professions, guaranteeing their success as chefs and their beneficial impact on the culinary community and the world.

A kitchen is a highly efficient system where every member has a vital function in creating a meal. Implementing discipline within a team facilitates effective coordination and communication, cultivating an environment characterized by mutual respect and friendship. The kitchen's effectiveness relies heavily on this shared commitment, particularly during busy periods when collaboration and effective communication are crucial in avoiding mistakes and delays.

The meticulousness of chefs and their culinary staff greatly influences each diner's experience, elevating an essential meal into a memorable interaction with food. The observed alteration is not a mere coincidence but a consequence of extensive training, emotional commitment, and steadfast devotion to the utmost standards of culinary prowess. To have a comprehensive understanding of the effect of culinary expertise on the dining experience, it is essential to thoroughly examine the several facets of the dining experience that are shaped by this field of study.

The field encompasses the process of choosing and managing components. Chefs that adhere to a rigorous methodology prioritize the quality and freshness of the ingredients used. The careful selection procedure guarantees the preservation and enhancement of the natural tastes of the foods, enabling guests to enjoy the essence of each piece of their dish fully. Cultivating reverence for foodstuffs via the application of rigorous standards also facilitates the adoption of sustainable and ethical culinary methodologies, harmonizing the dining encounter with the increasing worldwide awareness of food origins and ecological consequences.

In addition to the food itself, the level of discipline has an impact on the atmosphere of the dining setting and the quality of service. An orderly kitchen and service personnel collaborate seamlessly to provide an ambiance that enhances the culinary offerings. The meticulousness shown in the design and arrangement of the eating area, the illumination, the auditory elements, and even the thermal conditions contribute to creating a meticulously crafted dining ambiance that amplifies total satisfaction. Guided by a consistent degree of rigor, the service achieves a smooth, attentive, and customized experience, fostering a sense of value and attentiveness among guests.

Furthermore, the culinary arts field serves as a cultural manifestation and interchange conduit. Chefs assume the role of cultural cuisine ambassadors by engaging in rigorous research and practical application of many culinary traditions. The eating experience serves as a conduit that facilitates the connection between diners and many cultures and customs from around the globe. The cultural interchange enhances the diner's comprehension and admiration of diverse culinary traditions worldwide, cultivating a feeling of global interconnectedness and collective human experience via the universally understood cuisine medium.

The culinary realm, characterized by its diverse range of tastes, textures, and scents, serves as a monument to the innovative mindset of those who reside inside its culinary spaces. However, hidden under the facade of this imaginative mixture sits a fundamental component often eclipsed by the brightness of originality and style: self-control. Within culinary artistry, discipline refers to the meticulous adherence to established standards, the unwavering pursuit of exceptional quality, and the systematic approach to fostering creativity that chefs and culinary experts must exemplify. This inquiry examines the crucial role of discipline in developing culinary skills, influencing not only the meals served on our tables but also the fundamental nature of the culinary arts.

The development of a chef's culinary personality is significantly influenced by the presence of discipline. Chefs acquire their own culinary expression, a distinctive style that sets their meals apart, by engaging in rigorous experimentation and continuous improvement. The concept of identity is not fixed but rather undergoes transformation as time progresses, with the incorporation of new abilities, methods, and influences being guided by a sense of discipline.

The food sector has a dynamic nature, whereby trends and preferences undergo quick evolution. The practice of discipline provides cooks with the necessary skills to effectively navigate and adapt to these changes. Chefs may effectively respond to evolving demands and preserve the integrity of their craft by demonstrating unwavering dedication to ongoing education and upholding rigorous standards.

Discipline transcends the realm of the person and exerts influence on the trajectory of the culinary arts by means of mentoring. Experienced culinary professionals not only transmit technical expertise to their apprentices but also inculcate the principles of self-control, diligence, and commitment. The transfer of information and values is essential for the ongoing development of culinary expertise, guaranteeing that the principles that form the foundation of current culinary accomplishments will guide future advancements.

The systematic methodology used in culinary artistry has extensive implications, including the contentment of patrons, the standing of institutions, and the advancement of the culinary arts as a whole. The use of discipline in the kitchen guarantees that each meal not only adheres to the chef's rigorous criteria but also enhances the whole eating experience, resulting in a memorable and transforming encounter. Furthermore, the cultivation of self-control inside the confines of the kitchen has a significant impact on the wider culinary sphere, fostering a climate of exceptional quality and ongoing development.

Focus is the second component of D.F.C is equally essential. In the kitchen, it is the capacity to focus all of one's energy and focus on the task. It could be in the exact preparation of recipes, the exquisite plating of food, or managing a bustling kitchen during peak times. Chefs who can focus with lasers allow for an intense engagement with their work, which leads to greater levels of creativity and innovation as well as excellence in their meals. This concentration level will enable chefs to stretch the limits of traditional cooking and discover new culinary horizons. For establishments, a well-organized team is one in which every member is aligned with the

The Other Five Senses

restaurant's vision and works to achieve these goals. This ensures that all aspects of dining, from the ambiance to the service and even meals, are carefully designed to align with the most high-quality expectations.

In the culinary world, focus isn't just an activity but a form. It is an essential element that separates extraordinary culinary experiences from regular ones. The art of precision in cooking and focus, grounded in the fundamentals of focus, lets chefs and professionals in the field master the complexity of their profession with grace and awe.

The path to mastering the art of cooking with precision starts with realizing that the focus is the lens through which chefs see their food ingredients, recipes, and techniques for cooking. It's an experience transcending the simple culinary process, becoming a concert of tastes, textures, and scents. Suppose a cook is entirely focused on the task at hand. In that case, everything - from the choice of the finest ingredients to the precise preparation of a recipe -- is executed with great accuracy and precision.

A kitchen is a place where focus requires a unique blend of focus as well as an intense involvement in the process of cooking. Chefs need to be in the moment and focused on the task in front of them, whether it's the delicate blend of the flavors that go into a sauce or the exact timing required to accomplish an ideal sear for a slice of meat. This focus ensures that every dish is prepared carefully, expressing the chef's vision and expertise.

Additionally, the art of cooking with accuracy is apparent when chefs handle a skillful kitchen's chaotic and hectic atmosphere. Maintaining focus amidst the flurry of activity--coordinating with the kitchen staff, keeping track of cooking times, and ensuring the quality of every plate that leaves the kitchen-- sets apart the truly skilled professionals. The high-pressure work environment requires not just technical expertise but also mental strength to keep a sharp eye on the end goal of creating an unforgettable dining experience.

The importance of focusing goes beyond the traditional recipes. It's equally essential in the world of creative and innovative cooking. When chefs experiment with new tastes, techniques, styles, and displays, it is the focus that they build upon the explorations of their cuisine. This allows them to explore confidently, being confident that adhering to the rules of accuracy will aid them in the trials and errors of creativity. This inventive process, supported by a disciplined approach, can lead to new dishes that test the boundaries of traditional cuisine and excite the senses.

Focus is also a crucial part of the mentoring and training of young culinary talents. Professional chefs can impart technical abilities and emphasize the importance of maintaining concentration when working in the kitchen. With their benefit, new chefs are taught to tackle their work with the same determination and precision, recognizing that focus is crucial to mastering complicated techniques and attaining perfection in the kitchen.

The art of cooking with precision, founded on concentration, is a testament to the passion and discipline that are the hallmarks of the culinary profession. It's a reminder that cooking isn't just mechanical but an expressive art that requires active participation from the chef. In the world of culinary standards that remain high and the pursuit of innovation is never-ending, the ability to concentrate and truly engage within the cooking process is an essential quality for any chef who wants to achieve excellence.

The Other Five Senses

The art of cooking with precision is a multifaceted idea that covers all aspects of the process, from the initial choice of ingredients to the final dish presentation. It requires a profound understanding of the basic principles of food preparation, a constant commitment to perfection, and, most importantly, being able to concentrate entirely on the task. This isn't only an essential competence need, but it's an obsession that drives their imagination and innovations and allows them always to surpass those expectations set by their customers. As the food world constantly evolves, focus and precision must be crucial to creating exceptional food experiences and capturing the essence and spirit of accurate culinary expertise.

Within the domain of culinary arts, two fundamental principles serve as the bedrock for achieving exceptional outcomes: concentration and uniformity. Although straightforward, these principles have significant implications in their implementation inside kitchens, ranging from modest households to upscale dining establishments. Their significance cannot be exaggerated, as they form the basis of culinary triumph, influencing every meal that emerges from a kitchen.

In the realm of culinary arts, the quality of concentration is advantageous and an essential foundation for achieving gourmet perfection. This theory, while seeming simple, involves an intricate interaction of cognitive, physiological, and affective factors, all of which contribute to the skill and achievement of a chef's culinary creations. To fully understand the fundamental significance of concentration in culinary pursuits, it is necessary to thoroughly explore its complex characteristics and carefully study its influence on all aspects of cooking, ranging from the choice of ingredients to the final presentation that enhances the dining experience.

The critical aspect of culinary concentration is in the chef's ability to channel their whole self into the production of food that conveys a narrative, elicits emotions, and satisfies the taste buds. This necessitates an unmatched degree of attentiveness, a condition in which the intellect and the senses become highly sensitive to the current job. The task of slicing herbs rhythmically, adjusting heat with great care, or drizzling a sauce artistically is executed with a profound reverence for the materials and the cooking procedure. This deep respect guarantees that every dish element is treated with meticulousness, accuracy, and purpose, establishing the basis for exceptional culinary creations.

Although concentration may evoke associations with monotony and inflexibility, within the culinary arts realm, it is a catalyst for fostering creativity and innovation. The cognitive faculties of a chef serve as a conducive environment for cultivating culinary creativity, enabling them to explore diverse tastes, textures, and methodologies that challenge conventional culinary practices. The process of creative emancipation is not disorderly but rather directed by the systematic implementation of concentration, guaranteeing that every novel concept is examined meticulously and with a commitment to achieving the highest standards. The outcome is a continuous progression of culinary craftsmanship, whereby conventional cuisine is reinterpreted, and novel masterpieces emerge, owing to the unwavering concentration of forward-thinking chefs.

The attainment of culinary excellence is contingent upon acquiring several methods, each requiring a certain concentration level. Proficiency in specific culinary skills, such as tempering chocolate and kneading bread, is attained through dedicated and focused practice. The chef's dedication to refining these methods is comparable to a musician's mastery of their scales; it is the fundamental basis for all other aspects. The unwavering commitment to achieving technical proficiency guarantees that each element of a culinary creation, regardless of its size or insignificance, is done with meticulousness and expertise, enhancing the overall coherence and equilibrium of the ultimate presentation.

The ultimate assessment of a chef's concentration is when the intensity is physically and metaphorically heightened. Amidst the tumultuous environment of a bustling kitchen, where many orders are accumulating, and the pursuit of flawlessness is imminent, the capacity to sustain concentration is the distinguishing factor between the competent and the exceptional. The demanding nature of this high-pressure setting necessitates the possession of technical expertise and innovation and the mental resilience to maintain composure. The chef adeptly manages the current situation, skillfully coordinating various tasks into a harmonious display of culinary prowess. During these instances, the power of concentration becomes evident, converting possible disorder into a harmonious display of effectiveness and creativity.

Attaining and sustaining concentration in the culinary domain is not a fixed objective but a fluid progression that develops during a chef's professional journey. Continuous learning, self-reflection, and adaptability are essential components in this process. Utilizing mindfulness, meditation, and visualization techniques is progressively acknowledged as a valuable strategy for augmenting concentration, enabling chefs to refine their cognitive abilities with their culinary expertise. Moreover, establishing a conducive kitchen environment, wherein the concentration is esteemed and promoted, is pivotal in fostering the forthcoming cohort of dedicated culinary practitioners.

The ramifications of concentration transcend the individual chef and their culinary creations, exerting influence on the whole culinary environment. Chefs that are dedicated to quality can encourage their staff, raise industry standards, and enhance the eating culture. They serve as a reminder that cooking, in its finest form, is not only a mechanical procedure but an artistic expression—a means by which enthusiasm, ingenuity, and concentration materialize in the culinary creations that adorn our dining surfaces.

Concentration also guarantees uniformity in the culinary field, a characteristic that is equally crucial to ingenuity. In the demanding setting of a professional kitchen, the capacity to consistently provide exceptional outcomes in different situations is of utmost importance. This necessitates a meticulous emphasis on every aspect, ranging from the careful choice of ingredients to the precise timing and flawless execution of every stage in the culinary procedure. The establishment of a restaurant's reputation for quality and dependability is facilitated by the consistency attained via focus, which fosters confidence among guests.

Focus is also essential in time management and multitasking. In a dynamic and fast-paced environment, multiple tasks must be coordinated simultaneously. Focused chefs can manage their time efficiently, prioritize tasks effectively, and remain calm under pressure. This focused approach ensures the kitchen runs smoothly and sets a positive mood for all the staff.

Focus is also essential to a chef's personal and professional development. The culinary world constantly evolves, with new ingredients, techniques, and trends always appearing. It would help if you were committed to lifelong experimentation and learning to stay relevant and innovative. It is essential to improve existing skills and knowledge and embrace new challenges and growth opportunities. A chef focused on their craft always tries to improve their skills and expand their knowledge.

Focus extends its influence beyond the chef and affects the entire culinary team. Focused kitchens are harmonious, with each team member aligned and engaged in the goal of creating outstanding meals. This synergy enhances the kitchen's efficiency and productivity and creates a positive work environment.

Focus is an essential element in the development of culinary craft. The culinary arts are defined by the skills, techniques, and creative processes they encompass. Focus is evident in all aspects of the culinary arts, from preparing ingredients to their final presentation. Focus allows chefs to master their craft and innovate with purpose. It also helps them deliver consistently delicious culinary experiences. Focus is a discipline and a passion for a chef, and it drives them to explore and share the infinite possibilities that food offers.

The essence of culinary concentration is in the intimate and personal link between the chef and their job. This relationship encompasses more than just the act of cooking; it involves comprehending the narrative behind each ingredient, the scientific principles behind each method, and the capacity to transform the ordinary into something absolutely exceptional. The concentrated involvement of chefs allows them to surpass the ordinary, create new ideas, and convey their individuality via the art of cooking.

Consistency is like the steady, quiet rhythm supporting a symphony in culinary arts. It's often overlooked, but it's integral to the harmony. Consistency is a measure of reliability and a cornerstone to elevate the culinary experience. This exploration explores consistency's nuanced roles in shaping chefs and dishes and the dining experience. It weaves through the intricacies of culinary practice to reveal how this principle becomes at the heart of culinary art.

Consistency, the third pillar of D.F.C., ensures that the highest standards established by discipline and focus are maintained daily. For a chef, consistency means that the food offered to every client at any time is of identical quality. This kind of consistency helps build a chef's credibility and creates customer confidence. When it comes to a dining establishment, consistency assures customers of a consistent and excellent experience each time they go. To attain this consistency requires regular training, precise standard operating procedures, and an environment of excellence that is embraced at every aspect of the company. It's about replicating the success of every meal, day after day, regardless of the unpredictable variables inherent to running a restaurant business.

Consistency, as a pillar of the culinary arts, is a complicated blend of science, artistry, and discipline. The constant search for excellence and uniformity is the foundation of the integrity of the profession and its achievement. In the culinary industry, consistency goes beyond repeating the same process, and it's about acquiring the capability to produce exceptional quality under any condition. The commitment to consistency is evident in each aspect of the industry, from selecting ingredients to serving the dish.

The essence of consistency in the culinary field is all about trust. Customers who visit a dining establishment have expectations based on their experience. Whether it's a basic café that serves coffee and cakes or a posh restaurant that offers an extensive tasting menu, Customers expect the same level of service and satisfaction. Every visit must exceed or meet customers' expectations, transforming occasional customers into long-term patrons. In this way, consistency is directly tied to the brand's reputation and its longevity of growth.

The process of achieving consistency in food starts by examining the components. Quality dishes demand high-end ingredients. Chefs must ensure that their products, meats, and other ingredients meet high standards. This usually involves establishing solid relationships with suppliers and knowing the subtleties of seasonality and the sources. Chefs must be flexible to ingredients' quality and availability changes while adjusting their methods and recipes to ensure consistency in their final product.

Education and training are crucial aspects in ensuring sameness. Professionals who work in the culinary field must have an understanding of the cooking process techniques, as well as the behavior of ingredients under various conditions. This helps them recreate dishes precisely, modify them to the changing conditions, and resolve problems that might compromise the quality. Continuous learning and adapting are critical as cooking techniques change and new ingredients are introduced.

Standardized procedures are a further pillar of consistency. These rules favor an outline for each chore at the table, from simple preparation to the final plating of dishes. They assure that everyone on the team of chefs, no matter their position or level of experience, is aware of the steps needed for them to obtain the desired result. Standardization can also benefit education and quality control, making detecting and correcting deviations from the expected standards easier.

However, despite its importance, keeping consistency is among the biggest challenges facing the food world. Kitchens are dynamic and are subject to a variety of external demands. Busy service times, staff turnover, and even the daily fluctuations in the quality of ingredients can affect the consistency of food created. Chefs and their teams must be proficient in tackling these issues, using expertise and flexibility to ensure the highest standards.

Innovation and technology have become valuable tools for the pursuit of consistency. Innovative cooking techniques, high-end tools, and data-driven solutions to menu creation and ingredient management are assisting chefs in accomplishing more consistent outcomes. These techniques enhance traditional skills, giving chefs new ways to improve their skills and create extraordinary dining experiences.

Consistency goes far beyond the kitchens and meals it prepares. It covers every aspect of the dining experience, such as service, ambiance, and customer experience. These aspects must be handled carefully to ensure they add to customers' perception of the establishment's quality and reliability. Staff training, interior design, and even defining the menu language all affect customers' degree of consistency.

The Other Five Senses

In a larger sense, consistency plays a vital part in defining and maintaining the culinary tradition. When they adhere to the traditional methods and recipes, chefs can contribute to the narrative of a particular cuisine and ensure that the unique tastes and traditions are handed down from generation to generation. However, the consistency of a recipe doesn't mean it is impossible to be creative. Many chefs use their understanding of traditional recipes to create a basis for their innovation, experimenting with new techniques and ingredients while maintaining a constant connection to the tradition of cooking that influenced them.

Consistency is a key to food reliability. A principle that requires focus on the details, a profound knowledge of the craft, and an unwavering dedication to the highest standards. It's a demanding but rewarding process, one that differentiates the desirable professionals in the field of culinary. With consistent practice, chefs and establishments get the respect and trust of their customers and can also help create the rich tapestry of international culinary culture. Pursuing consistency is a never-ending journey, a continual cycle of adaptation, learning, and improvement vital to the culinary arts' dynamism and vitality.

Primarily, the meticulousness in culinary implementation, stemming directly from self-control, guarantees that each meal presented is a work of art. The chef's meticulous approach is evident in the same taste, texture, and temperature throughout all portions. The degree of uniformity is what patrons develop confidence in and anticipate, resulting in recurring visits and a devoted clientele. The level of accuracy extends beyond the gustatory experience. It involves the visual presentation of the culinary creation, which often serves as the first point of contact between the customer and their food. An exquisitely presented meal, meticulously arranged, establishes the ambiance for the dining encounter, guaranteeing a culinary journey that is often as visually captivating as delectable.

Within the realm of culinary arts, the concept of "consistency" has a significance beyond the straightforwardness of its description. To those unfamiliar, it may imply the repetition of chores or the capacity to reproduce a particular cuisine. Nevertheless, in the dynamic settings of kitchens, ranging from modest caféés to opulent dining facilities, maintaining consistency is the fundamental basis for establishing culinary dependability. This comprehensive investigation examines the complex and diverse aspects of consistency within the culinary domain, shedding light on its importance, its difficulties, and the approaches experts use to attain it.

The concept of consistency in the culinary realm extends beyond the simple duplication of a dish's taste characteristics or visual appeal. The concept involves a comprehensive approach to the dining experience, whereby every aspect, including the atmosphere, service, and the quality and presentation of the cuisine, plays a role in creating a cohesive and unforgettable dinner. Consistency serves as the fundamental element that unifies the essence of a restaurant's character, setting it apart in a highly competitive environment and fostering a devoted customer base.

Attaining and sustaining consistency is a task filled with difficulties. The diversity of ingredients, the intricacies of human expertise and interaction, and the ever-changing nature of culinary tastes all contribute to the difficulty of achieving consistency. The quality and features of ingredients may exhibit variation throughout several batches, while culinary methods need a gradual refinement of accuracy and competence. Additionally, diner tastes are subject to change, affected by prevailing trends and personal experiences. These factors require a diligent and flexible approach to the administration of culinary operations.

The establishment of culinary consistency is predicated upon the acquisition of expertise in both ingredients and processes. Chefs dedicate extensive time to acquiring expertise in ingredient selection, comprehending their characteristics, and adjusting to their variations. This acquired knowledge allows individuals to make necessary modifications that guarantee the final meal adheres to the intended quality, irrespective of the inherent variations in the raw components. In the same vein, mastering culinary methods enables chefs to meticulously carry out recipes, guaranteeing the constant preparation of every element inside a meal.

The attainment of consistency is not just the duty of the head chef but rather necessitates the collaborative effort of the whole kitchen staff. Thorough training programs are crucial to provide each team member with the necessary skills and knowledge to carry out their tasks consistently. This training extends beyond technical proficiency, including elements of collaboration, effective communication, and the capacity to foresee and adjust to obstacles. Maintaining consistency necessitates the presence of a cohesive team, whereby each member has a comprehensive understanding of their roles and contributions to the overall experience.

Systems and procedures play a crucial role in maintaining consistency within the changing environment of a kitchen. Examples of systems that contribute to the maintenance of uniformity include standardized recipes, exact measurement and preparation processes, and consistent plating requirements. In addition, inventory management methods play a crucial role in maintaining constant ingredient quality, while workflow management solutions are designed to enhance efficiency and reduce mistakes.

Achieving consistency is a continuous process of acquiring knowledge and adjusting accordingly. Culinary professionals consistently solicit input from patrons, colleagues, and critics to get insights into potential areas of improvement. By implementing a feedback loop and fostering a culture of ongoing enhancement, restaurants can enhance their products and adjust to evolving tastes and preferences while maintaining the fundamental stability that customers depend on.

The advantages associated with attaining consistency extend far beyond the realm of consumer happiness. Establishing a restaurant's reputation, cultivating customer loyalty, and achieving financial stability are all significantly influenced by its essential function. The establishment's ability to maintain a high standard of quality and service fosters a sense of trust among its customers, promoting customer loyalty and positive word-of-mouth referrals. Moreover, maintaining uniformity in operations and implementation may result in enhanced efficiency and cost control, bolstering the business's general prosperity and durability.

Within the realm of culinary arts, the concept of consistency extends beyond the mere replication of tastes or presentations, including the notions of dependability and trust. Customers often revisit dining venues that consistently provide their preferred dishes, ensuring that their expectations are consistently met. Attaining such a high level of consistency is a formidable challenge, requiring chefs to demonstrate unwavering dedication to the exact execution of duties on a daily basis.

The act of engaging in repeated practice extends beyond the simple performance of tasks, as it encompasses a contemplative procedure that enables chefs to develop a profound comprehension of their ingredients and skills. Chefs have the ability to adapt instinctively to fluctuations in ingredient quality or kitchen dynamics via repeated practice, so guaranteeing that every dish they produce serves as a tribute to their unwavering dedication to achieving exceptional standards. This facet of self-control has both positive and negative implications; it requires persistence while also offering the potential benefits of expertise and self-assurance in one's chosen field.

In addition to technical development, the cultivation of attention assumes a pivotal part in the creative process of formulating novel culinary creations and menus. Culinary innovation is not a haphazard manifestation of inspiration but rather a deliberate investigation into the intricacies of tastes, textures, and visual elements. The process entails a deliberate examination of the interplay between various components of culinary creation, their reception by the consumer, and their contribution to the holistic gastronomic encounter. The creative process requires a high degree of concentration that is both rigorous and broad-minded, enabling chefs to challenge conventional culinary methods and go into uncharted territories.

The pursuit of excellence is at the heart of culinary art, and it's deeply intertwined with consistency. Chefs begin their journey to mastery with foundational skills, such as precise knife cuts, delicate flavors, and meticulous timing. Consistency is the key to success and requires repetition and discipline. It is a rigorous process that requires countless hours to perfect.

However, consistency in skill development is only one aspect of its importance in culinary craftsmanship. Chefs progress as they explore various culinary techniques, ingredients, and traditions. Here, consistency becomes a tool to explore and innovate. Understanding the intrinsic qualities of ingredients and their interactions and applying that knowledge consistently allows chefs to push the boundaries of their dishes while maintaining their integrity. The balance between innovation, reliability, and quality is delicate. Consistency acts as the fulcrum to allow chefs to explore new horizons while maintaining the standards and quality that define their craft.

Consistency is the key to a professional kitchen's service. Good chefs are distinguished by their ability to consistently produce high-quality dishes, regardless of pressures or dynamics in service. Achieving this level of consistency requires individual discipline and skill and a team working together towards a shared goal. In essence, the kitchen is a symphony with many moving parts. Consistency in execution is critical to ensuring that every service meets the high standards of discerning diners.

Consistency is also a significant factor in developing a chef's signature. Chefs create their signature style by refining their skills and exploring new culinary interests. In this context, consistency is maintaining a cohesive identity across menus and dishes to allow diners to experience and appreciate the unique culinary perspective of the chef. This identity does not remain static but instead evolves with time. Consistency ensures that this evolution stays true to the principles and values of the culinary philosophy.

Consistency is essential in the dining room as well as the kitchen. It shapes the entire dining experience. Consistency in service, quality, and ambiance creates trust and loyalty among diners. It's the assurance that every visit will be just as pleasant as the previous one, which creates a bond between diner and establishment. Consistency is a critical differentiator in a world where diners are spoiled for choice. It gives them a reason to come back to a restaurant.

Consistency is also crucial in the training and mentoring of the next-generation chefs. When imparting their knowledge and skills to the next generation of chefs, experienced chefs stress the importance and discipline required for excellence. Mentorship is essential to ensure that principles of consistency, craftsmanship, and integrity are passed on to the future of culinary arts.

The challenges to maintaining consistency are many. Maintaining consistency is a constant battle against change, from the variations of ingredients to the dynamic of the kitchen staff. It takes adaptability and resilience. Chefs develop these qualities over time as they learn to navigate through the uncertainty of the culinary world. Consistency is not only about maintaining standards but also about continuous improvement and growth.

Consistency is the foundation of any business in the culinary world. Consistency is the basis on which companies build and grow their reputation. Consistency in food quality, service level, and overall dining experience are what restaurants use to attract and retain customers. Consistency is even more critical in an age where social media and online reviews can significantly impact a restaurant's performance. It acts as a buffer to the volatile public opinion.

Consistency is a multifaceted aspect of culinary art. It's a principle that demands respect, discipline and dedication. It challenges chefs to strive for excellence. Consistency allows culinary art to flourish and fosters a culture of culinary excellence. Consistency is the thread that ties together all the elements of culinary art, from the preparation of the ingredients to the presentation of the dish.

Consistency is not just a characteristic; it's a principle at the core of culinary arts. Consistency allows chefs to refine their craft and confidently express their culinary visions. Consistency is critical to developing culinary skills. It's through consistency that culinary art reaches its highest expression and leaves a lasting impression on the culinary landscape.

The cumulative impact of D.F.C on the culinary profession is significant. Chefs who follow these guidelines make a mark in a competitive industry. They are more likely to get acknowledged and valued by the people who matter, whether those who eat, the critics, or even potential employers. The ability to master D.F.C opens the door to job advancement, ranging from possibilities to being employed in elegant kitchens and invitations to take part in food and beverage showcases worldwide. It also allows chefs to create their own brand identities, with a distinctive culinary style and reputation for quality. The personal brand is an asset that opens the way for many well-qualified opportunities, such as consulting positions, media appearances, and entrepreneurial ventures within food and drink.

The advantages of adopting D.F.C are just as significant for restaurants that cater to customers. Cafes, restaurants, and other businesses that deal with food and operate according to these principles experience greater appreciation and satisfaction. The reason for this is that diners appreciate not only the quality of food but also the whole dining experience, which is enhanced through their discipline, focus, and the pureness of the staff behind it. In addition, establishments that adhere to D.F.C tend to recruit and retain skilled professionals who share these values. This will, in turn, create an atmosphere of excellence, increasing the establishment's credibility regarding operational efficiency and financial viability. It is a competitive field in which new businesses constantly compete for attention. Being recognized for constant discipline, focused attention to detail, and continuous quality is a crucial element to stand out and succeed.

D.F.C also plays an essential role in how establishments handle and respond to changing circumstances. The discipline needed to maintain top standards, the determination to solve problems effectively, and the rigor to warrant stability through change are essential in navigating the peaks and valleys of the food business. It doesn't matter if it's adapting to the latest trends in food, responding to customers' needs, or facing operational hurdles; establishments that are a part of D.F.C. are more able to adapt and grow with a sustainable approach.

The effect of discipline, focus, and consistency in the culinary profession and establishments is omnipresent. These rules outline individual and organizational success and are the foundation of the dining experience. They warrant that each meal served and every dining experience is a tribute to the effort, determination, passion, and dedication of all those working in the food industry. This is why D.F.C is the foundation of culinary excellence, pushing forward the field and improving the science and art of cooking to new heights.

In the culinary arts discipline, focus and consistency are more than words. They are the guiding principles that lead chefs and professionals to pursue perfection. They require more than just an understanding of cooking methods and ingredients but also a commitment to personal and well-qualified improvement. Becoming a D.F.C. is not easy and requires determination, perseverance, and dedication. However, the rewards- personal happiness, competent recognition, and the pleasure of creating unforgettable culinary experiences- are worth the time and effort. While the world of food is constantly evolving, the fundamentals of D.F.C remain the same, emphasizing the science, art, and the heart of cooking. This examination of D.F.C in the realm of culinary highlights its crucial contribution to shaping careers, creating establishments, and elevating dining experiences. Professionals in the culinary field who live by these ideals stand out in the diverse and rich array of the world's culinary world.

The consequences of not developing discipline, focus, and consistency can affect the chef's personal growth and career success and the quality they deliver in the dining room. What could happen if each quality is missing?

Lack of focus may lead to mistakes in recipes, such as wrong measurements, forgotten ingredients, or incorrect timing of cooking processes. These errors can compromise the taste and appearance of dishes. Cooking is dangerous because it involves using sharp objects and hot surfaces. Accidents and injuries can occur if you are not paying attention. This puts the cook and everyone else in the kitchen at risk.

The Other Five Senses

Concentration is crucial to creativity in cooking. Without it, a chef may find it challenging to innovate and bring new ideas to fruition. This can lead to a stagnant menu.

Discipline is the key to learning and improving. Cooks may be unable to improve their skills or master new techniques without discipline.

Consistency in quality is impossible without discipline. Discipline can lead to a fluctuating standard, with daily dishes that vary in taste and appearance.

Unreliable Work Ethics: A disciplined work ethic ensures that tasks will be completed efficiently and effectively. A cook lacking discipline may have difficulty managing time, miss deadlines, or not adequately prepare for service. This can negatively impact the kitchen's operations.

Eroded trust with diners: When visiting a restaurant, diners expect to receive a certain standard of service and quality. Consistency can lead to customers being disappointed and leaving negative reviews.

Lack of cohesion within the team: By following procedures and recipes consistently, all members can work together seamlessly. It can lead to confusion and discord between staff members, affecting service quality.

Career Limitation: Chefs, cooks, and restaurateurs build their reputations based on the consistency of their culinary creations. Inconsistency may limit professional opportunities and hinder advancement in the culinary world.

A lack of focus, consistency, and discipline can affect a cook's career. This can make it hard to develop a professional or personal identity in the culinary industry and even harder to stand out. A cook lacking these qualities may struggle to find personal satisfaction and motivation as culinary success becomes more difficult.

The dynamic and collaborative nature of the kitchen demands that these qualities be developed not only for the individual's success but also for the entire team's success. Failure to maintain focus, discipline, and consistency may affect relationships with co-workers, team morale, and, ultimately, the dining experience provided to guests.

Developing discipline, focus, and consistency is essential for anyone who wants to excel at their craft, especially in the dynamic and demanding world of culinary arts. These qualities can be developed and strengthened by deliberate effort and practice. While they may come naturally to some people, it is also possible for them to create and maintain. These are some steps you can take to improve these qualities.

Focus, discipline, and consistency can be developed through deliberate effort, dedication, and perseverance. Individuals can unlock their potential and enhance their abilities by setting clear goals, practicing mindfulness techniques and concentration, creating structured routines, adopting continuous learning and improvements, cultivating self-discipline, and creating supportive environments. Through constant practice, reflection, and adjustment, these qualities will become ingrained in the individual's mind, leading them to success and fulfillment in their personal and professional lives.

CHAPTER SIX

A Sense of Humor

When you consider the culinary arts, the first aspect that might come to mind is the meticulous crafting of terrific dishes, appropriate timing, and the cautious balancing of flavors. What might not come to mind right away is humor. Yet, everyone who has ever stepped at the back of the stove with a recipe in hand is aware that cooking, like life, is often quality approached with an excellent dose of laughter.

Consider the humble soufflé, a dish infamous for its temperamental nature. The stakes are excessive; the anxiety inside the kitchen could be reduced with a knife—literally and figuratively. Now, imagine drawing near this culinary assignment with the seriousness of a coronary heart physician. The eggs are whipped, the oven preheated, and the atmosphere is so disturbing you would possibly neglect that what you're making is essentially a glorified omelet. In these excessive-tension moments, humorousness isn't just beneficial; it's critical. Laughing off a fallen soufflé can be the difference between an amusing nighttime and a culinary catastrophe. After all, you may always strive again, and maybe the following will rise to the occasion.

Cooking, a serene artwork, frequently performs as a dramatic event inside the kitchen's heat. Whether you are a pro chef or a domestic chef preparing dinner, the kitchen does now not discriminate about ability disasters. But what if we approached them with humor rather than fretting over these kitchen mishaps? It's about reworking the kitchen from a battlefield to a playground, where every mistake isn't always a setback but a hazard for creative expression and an excellent snigger.

Imagine you are hosting a dinner party. You've deliberated the whole thing meticulously, from a three course meal to the correct playlist. As the principle sauce simmers on the range, you open the oven to locate that your superbly expected soufflé has collapsed into an unhappy puddle. It's a culinary nightmare for plenty, but here lies a preference—sink into despair or snicker it off and serve it with a witty remark about "deconstructed delicacies." More often than not, your visitors will recognize the humor (and the honesty) more than a perfect dish. They'll not forget the laughter that stuffed your dining room long after forgetting what they ate.

This method isn't always making mild of our efforts in the kitchen but about lightening the weight that often comes with culinary expectancies. Take Julia Child, one of the most revered chefs and television personalities, who famously dropped a turkey on the floor through her show. Without lacking a beat, she picked it up and reassured her target market that their visitors would never recognize it if they were alone in the kitchen. This moment, packed with unscripted humor, endeared Julia even more to her target audience. It wasn't just her cooking skills but her ability to gracefully deal with mistakes with humor that won the hearts of many.

Humor in the kitchen also can be an effective coaching device. When expert cooks educate their kitchen staff, the surroundings may be severe. However, chefs who inject humor into their coaching regularly see higher outcomes. Their workforce is more comfortable, willing to take risks, and communicative. They analyze that errors aren't profession-enders but are a part of the culinary

The Other Five Senses

adventure. Like every cherished chef and creator, Anthony Bourdain embraced his mishaps and those of others with the same enthusiasm. His writings frequently reflect kitchen life's chaotic, absurd, and ultimately funny realities, making it clear that perfection isn't the purpose—ardor is.

For domestic cooks, this philosophy maybe even more releasing. Without the excessive stakes of a restaurant environment, the home kitchen can emerge as a lab for experimental cooking. Did your try at homemade pasta become a sticky mess? Turn it right into a risk to order from your favorite Italian region, joking about how your pasta is so authentic, it's invisible. Burnt the roast? Crack a joke about your new recipe for a "blackened, more crisp" delicacy. These moments can end up treasured own family testimonies, reminding each person that the kitchen is as an awful lot an area for laughter as it's miles for ingesting.

Moreover, embracing humor enables building resilience. Cooking includes many elements and variables, from unpredictable and fluctuating oven temperatures. By learning how to snort at matters that move wrong, cooks can shrug off frustrations and get better from setbacks without difficulty. This resilience can seep into different regions of existence, providing a more incredibly pleased and constructive outlook on the inevitable imperfections of daily living.

Social media has additionally amplified the attainment of kitchen humor. Platforms like Instagram and TikTok are full of cooking fails, in which customers proudly showcase their culinary screw-ups with a heavy dose of humor. These posts not only pass viral for their relate ability but additionally assist in constructing a community that cheers on culinary trials in preference to simply polished, perfect dishes. It's a collective acknowledgment that everybody makes errors and that there's a pleasure to be found in every misstep.

Through this lens, the kitchen transforms from a website of ability failure to a stage for improvisation and pleasure. Every burnt pie crust or over-salted soup isn't only a mishap; it's cloth for an excellent tale, a hearty snicker, and, most significantly, a learning enjoyment. It's approximately finding pleasure in the cooking journey, now not just the vacation spot at the plate. This method doesn't simply make cooking extra fun; it makes lifestyles more exciting, reminding us that perfection isn't always the best overrated but also much less delicious than a dish served with a facet of humor.

In culinary arts, improvisation isn't always a talent but an art. A chef needs to be bold, creative, and flexible. Every pro chef is aware of that now and then. The most memorable kitchen creations get up now not from meticulously following a recipe but from the spontaneous and regularly humorous deviations along the way. This is the essence of culinary improvisation—in which the sudden will become the name of the game element.

When you step into a kitchen, you input a realm where every component, every spice, and every utensil offers a potential for wonder. A missing ingredient or a wrong flip while following a recipe would not spell a disaster. Instead, it can be an invitation to innovate, an opportunity to inject a piece of persona into the dish. This system is not salvaging a meal but remodeling it into something uniquely pleasant. The position of humor here can't be overstated— it is the chef's ally, ensuring that the environment stays mild and that creativity flows freely.

The Other Five Senses

Take, for example, the tale of a chef who, in the middle of making ready an excessive-stakes dinner, found out he was out of basil, a key factor for his signature pasta sauce. Instead of panicking, he turned to mint, which became considerable in his lawn. The result? A refreshingly fragrant sauce that now not handiest complemented the pasta but has become the speak of the night. Guests have been amused and pleasantly amazed by using the radical desire, which the chef jovially dubbed "Minted Marinara Madness." This second of brief questioning not only stored the dish but also introduced an element of humor and tale that visitors remembered long after the remaining chew.

Humor in cooking also comes into play when chefs test with unconventional cooking methods. Imagine sluggish-cooking ribs in a dishwasher—a technique a few adventurous chefs have attempted with a wink and a nudge, wrapping the ribs tightly in foil and jogging them on an ordinary cycle. While it might increase eyebrows, the ribs pop out noticeably smooth. It's an unusual approach that's sure to inject some humor into any dinner verbal exchange. Such strategies won't emerge as trendy culinary practices. However, they highlight how a playful approach can cause modern cooking methods.

In professional kitchens, cooks frequently face the stress of delivering perfect dishes below tight cut-off dates. In such excessive-strain environments, humor turns into a crucial device. It's commonplace to hear laughter echoing through the kitchen as cooks jest about the chaos of a dinner rush or playfully compete with peers who can create the most bizarre dish using leftover substances. This humor isn't always just for entertainment; it builds camaraderie, fosters high-quality painting surroundings, and encourages creative dangers.

Moreover, culinary improvisation and humor go hand in hand inside the realm of fusion delicacies, in which the mixture of disparate culinary traditions can lead to unexpected and often laugh effects. A conventional example is the "cronut," a hybrid of a croissant and a doughnut, which became born out of a playful test and emerged directly as an international sensation. Such innovations exhibit how humor and creativity can break the boundaries of traditional delicacies, leading to new and exciting culinary experiences.

Even in domestic cooking, humor is necessary to make the kitchen a welcoming space for experimentation and pleasure. Families can interact in playful challenges, like developing the most colorful pizza or the strangest ice cream taste. These sports not only make cooking amusing but also assist in constructing lasting reminiscences. When kids see adults embracing mistakes and giggling off mishaps in the kitchen, they learn resilience and creativity, which are vital components for each cooking and existence.

The artwork of culinary improvisation is enriched with the aid of humorousness. It lets chefs and home chefs transcend traditional cooking techniques and create dishes that are not only delicious but also a mirror image of their playful spirit. This approach to cooking—wherein one is endorsed to chortle, experiment, and occasionally even fail—reminds us that the journey is as critical as the destination. It turns each cooking experience into a trip, wherein each misstep is a hazard for a new creation, and each dish tells the tale of a pleased, ingenious conquest inside the kitchen.

The Other Five Senses

More than just entertainment comedy in cooking shows serves a pivotal position past merely pleasing the audience; it transforms the kitchen from a daunting area of precise measurements and doubtlessly demanding results into a level for creativity, mishaps, and human connection. The integration of humor into cooking has made culinary arts more reachable and appreciably altered viewers' perceptions of cooking, turning it into a fun and approachable activity.

At the heart of the culinary television style, humor acts as a tremendous equalizer, demystifying the complexities of cooking. For many visitors, the kitchen represents a high-stakes environment where precision rules and errors are frowned upon. However, while chefs on screen meet those errors with humor instead of disdain, it sends a powerful message: it's miles k to make errors. This technique is essential as it humanizes cooks, making them more relatable. Viewers wondering, "If they could snort off a burnt pie, so can I," are much more likely to strive to cook themselves, fostering a getting-to-know surroundings that embraces flaws as part of the culinary adventure.

One quintessential instance of humor-infused cooking is observed inside the suggests of Julia Child. Known for her cheerful demeanor and occasional clumsiness, Child frequently dropped utensils, forgot components, or handled kitchen mishaps on air. Yet, it changed into her response—chuckling, shrugging, and shifting on—that endeared her to thousands and thousands. She famously quipped, "Never make an apology for cooking," which encapsulated her philosophy that the kitchen should be a place of joy and experimentation, now not perfectionism and fear.

Similarly, British chef Jamie Oliver brings a laid-back, jovial method to his cooking shows. His on-screen persona is that of a friend cooking beside you rather than a chef lecturing you. Oliver's humor and casual banter, regularly even as cutting onions or stirring a pot, assist in breaking down the barrier of intimidation many people experience in cooking. His capacity to snicker at himself while something would not cross as deliberate or his playful banter with components encourages visitors to see cooking as a fun pastime instead of a chore.

On the opposite quit of the spectrum is Gordon Ramsay, regarded for his fiery temper and sharp tongue on suggests like "Hell's Kitchen." However, even Ramsay's stern demeanor is laced with a type of humor—often dry and biting, but it serves to entertain and teach. His harsh evaluations, added with a dose of theatrical aptitude, are regularly punctuated with witty one-liners that now not most effectively lighten the mood but additionally make memorable teaching moments. Viewers would possibly mimic his grievance about their kitchens, guffawing at their culinary errors, which paradoxically encourages them to take cooking more seriously.

In recent years, the arrival of net personalities has further broadened the panorama of humorous cooking content. YouTubers and social media chefs frequently use humor in quick, relatable skits accompanying their recipes. This layout no longer draws a more youthful demographic but also caters to the fast interest spans prevalent, making cooking seem speedy, easy, and exciting. For example, YouTuber Rosanna Pansino blends humor with her love for nerdy cultures in her cooking series, developing themed treats that enchant lovers of diverse genres while retaining the temper light and festive.

The Other Five Senses

Humor in cooking shows regularly extends past the food, concerning cultural and private stories that add depth to the culinary enjoyment. Chefs like Eddie Huang and David Chang use humor to navigate the complexities in their cultural history through meals, sharing private anecdotes that might be both a laugh and insightful. This approach now entertains and enriches viewers' know-how of the range of culinary practices and the private connections that food can foster.

Comedy in cooking indicates more than just entertainment; it makes cooking available and relatable. It transforms the kitchen into a space where perfection is less important than entertainment and personal expression. By watching cooks who embrace humor, viewers now research the most effective way to cook dinner and how to enjoy the manner, guffawing on the flops and celebrating the successes. This evolution in culinary TV has made it clear that in the kitchen, as in life, a fantastic humorousness is just as important as a great knife.

At the heart of every memorable dining experience is the food and the atmosphere, wherein it's miles loved. Humor acts as the social spice, improving flavors on the palate and our interactions, making the eating table an area of connection and pleasure. As families acquire and friends convene, the kitchen and the eating room end up stages for shared laughter and entertainment. Hosts can rework even the maximum habitual gatherings into loved memories by weaving humor into meal guidance and presentation.

Dining together, especially during events or gatherings, can sometimes fire up underlying tensions—from meeting new people, discussing sensitive topics, or the austere strain of trying the meal to move ideally. Humor serves as a herbal diffuser of such anxiety, permitting people to loosen up in an instant. A properly-timed funny story or a playful dish presentation can smash the ice and ease guests' experience. For example, believe in serving a complicated risotto with a fanciful name like "Risotto of the Lost Ark" or presenting a child-friendly dish called "Dinosaur Nuggets inside the Jungle of Broccoli." These playful touches can turn apprehension into leisure, encouraging visitors to engage extra brazenly and warmly with each other.

Involving a circle of relatives individuals in cooking, mainly kids, gives a fertile floor for humorous interactions that decorate bonding. Whether the flour fights while baking cookies or the innovative, albeit messy, attempts at garnishing dishes, these moments are ripe for laughter. Such activities no longer amuse the cooking technique but also instill a sense of achievement and pleasure in kids, making them more keen to participate in future culinary ventures. Parents can capitalize on this by assigning humorous titles to kitchen obligations, including "Chief Egg Cracker" or "Veggie Whisperer," making mundane responsibilities like exciting adventures.

Traditions anchor our social interactions in familiarity and comfort, and introducing humorous traditions around eating can fortify these ties. This could be as easy as having a funny hat that the chef of the day wears or developing a ritual in which the worst dish of a potluck gets a playful, mock 'award.' Such traditions encourage participation and make each meal unique and eagerly anticipated. They additionally serve as extraordinary memories that one's family, individuals, or friends can reminisce about in future gatherings.

The presentation of meals offers a canvas for humor. Creative plating can turn dishes into visual puns or laugh scenes that provoke laughter and pleasure at the desk. For example, using sauces to attract smiley faces on pancakes or arranging veggies in a quirky, creative manner can make the dish extra attractive and instigate joyful interactions. These playful presentations can be particularly effective throughout celebrations or vacations, where subject matters can be more tricky, including ghost-formed mashed potatoes for Halloween or a turkey wearing a humorous dress for Thanksgiving.

Themed dinner nights are a brilliant way to inject humor into eating. Themes can be based on movies, historical durations, or even inside jokes amongst pals or their own family. For instance, a "Pirate Night" in which everybody speaks in pirate slang and the meals are served in treasure chests can offer a wholly immersive and laugh revel. Similarly, pairing foods with humorous, surprising names like "Belly Laugh Beaverbrook" or "Giggle Beans" can add a detail of marvel and joy to the meal.

Beyond simply enhancing the dining revel, humor has tangible mental blessings. Laughter triggers the discharge of endorphins, the frame's herbal feel-top chemical compounds. It promotes a usual experience of well-being and can even temporarily relieve pain. By making laughter part of the dining revel, hosts no longer only ensure pleasant nighttime but also contribute to the holistic fitness of their visitors. In this way, humor will now become not only a social device but a restoration one, fostering both emotional and bodily connectivity.

By prioritizing humor in meal guidance and presentation, what we create in the long run is more than just a meal—we forge an experience. It reveals wherein laughter mingles with the aromas of cooked spices, memories are shared with every chunk, and every accumulation leaves a lingering aftertaste of joy. In this light, humor is the most crucial aspect in the recipe for memorable eating, transforming the desk into a place of uninhibited pleasure and profound connection.

In culinary arts, the interaction between subculture and innovation is a delicate dance. While respecting time-venerated recipes is critical, introducing playful, humorous twists can rework an everyday meal practice into a fascinating and pleasant experience. This exploration delves into how infusing humor into traditional recipes no longer only keeps their integrity but also complements the general leisure of cooking.

Every culture boasts dishes that have stood the check of time, liked through generations for their flavors, stories, and the experience of identity they bestow. However, even the most sacred culinary traditions can benefit from a hint of lightheartedness. For example, recall the traditional French dish, coq au vin. Traditionally, this dish is an image of French culinary finesse concerning slow-cooking chicken in wine. Now, believe in renaming it to "Tipsy Chicken" for a more excellent informal dinner party. Such a whimsical twist now serves as an icebreaker, making this venerable dish more approachable and less daunting for novice chefs.

Another manner to inject a laugh into conventional recipes is through sudden aspect substitutions. These can add an element of marvel and personalize a dish to mirror contemporary tastes or dietary options. For example, changing the raisins in a traditional carrot cake with dried cranberries dyed green can create a visual gag about "carrot tops" while maintaining the dish's beloved texture and flavor intact.

The Other Five Senses

Turning the cooking technique into an interactive activity is a super way to make traditional cooking amusing. For instance, setting up a "taco bar" wherein visitors can bring together their tacos from loads of conventional and unconventional toppings provides an element of play to the meal. This makes the method more attractive and allows visitors to experiment with flavors and actively participate in introducing their food.

Integrating humor into traditional cooking is not about undermining the culinary arts but improving the leisure and communal enjoyment of cooking and consuming. By adapting recipes with playful shows, whimsical naming conventions, and interactive elements, we can breathe new existence into age-antique dishes and make the kitchen an area of joy and laughter. This technique now preserves the essence of conventional recipes and makes them more convenient and exciting for everyone, proving that laughter might be a pleasant ingredient even in cooking.

In any professional surroundings, whether or not in a bustling company office, a serene artist's studio, or a heated kitchen, the presence of humor is often seen as a double-edged sword. While it's miles universally stated that humor lightens the temper and fosters an adequate place of work environment, there persists an underlying query: Does having a sense of humor suggest that one does now not take one's obligations seriously? This discourse aims to unravel this misconception by exploring how humor can coexist with, and even enhance, extreme dedication to expert obligations throughout numerous fields.

When we communicate about humor in the administrative center, it's vital to understand that it goes beyond just making people snort. It involves a well-timed and appropriate expression of leisure that can relieve anxiety. For example, in high-stress conditions, a well-timed, mild-hearted remark can assist in diffusing anxiety, permitting team individuals to regain their composure and awareness of the task at hand. Moreover, humor can serve as a social lubricant, smoothing interactions like few other things. It can break down obstacles between hierarchical levels, encouraging an extra democratic environment wherein thoughts flow extra freely.

Moreover, humor improves communication by using shooting interest and growing in mind. Information presented humorously is much more likely to be remembered, which is especially beneficial in fields wherein many new records are constantly shared. Additionally, while leaders use humor, they frequently become more approachable, which could make employees feel extra comfortable sharing thoughts and worries. This openness can result in better hassle-solving and innovation as groups feel more assured of their creative questioning.

From a mental perspective, humor is a complicated social and cognitive procedure. It includes comprehension, appreciation, and the correct use of comedic elements. Cognitive theories of humor, which consist of the concept of contradiction, endorse that humor arises when there is a discrepancy between what is expected and what occurs. Still, this discrepancy wishes to be resolved in a manner that is non-threatening and sudden. Understanding a funny story or situation requires a complicated intellectual assignment of processing records, spotting these contradictions, and resolving them into coherent knowledge.

Resolving contradictions complements cognitive flexibility, which is crucial in expert settings. Cognitive flexibility includes the ability to modify one's questioning from old situations to new conditions, reflect on consideration of more than one idea simultaneously, and switch between exceptional minds as the state of affairs demands. In the administrative center, this capability complements problem-solving abilities and creativity. It permits employees to adapt to changing environments, think about unconventional answers to issues, and innovate.

Furthermore, the usage of humor has been linked to elevated resilience, which is the capability to cope with strain and adversity. By fostering a piece of surroundings that doesn't take itself too seriously, businesses can help employees correctly navigate challenging instances. This would not mean that the work itself isn't always taken severely, but as a substitute, the technique to work includes moments of lightness that make the load experience a piece lighter.

Far from being a trademark of a loss of seriousness, humor in professional settings can represent a relatively functioning cognitive technique. It suggests that personnel and leaders alike can suppose fast on their feet, admire the nuances of social interactions, and discover innovative solutions to issues. Indeed, the ability to humorously frame a state of affairs regularly calls for a deep knowledge of the context, the target market, and the timing—abilities that are worthwhile in any expert putting.

In essence, humor in expert settings is set stability. It approximately knows how to inject lightness to improve morale or aid comprehension while keeping seriousness to ensure that expert obligations and responsibilities are genuinely understood and acted upon. This stability is critical for maintaining surroundings that are fun and productive.

In professions with high stakes and the emotional toll that can be tremendous, humor is a necessary remedy. Medical specialists, for example, frequently work in environments wherein the road between existence and death is perilously skinny. Here, humor can be a way to retake a short step, breathe, and preserve the emotional and intellectual balance that has to be carried out below pressure. The ability to tell shaggy dog stories about the quirks of medical institution life or the peculiarities of day-by-day exercises can assist in building resilience and reducing burnout. This is not about making light of patients' suffering or the gravity of the scientific career but about keeping a level of detachment that is important to characteristics correctly day in and time out.

Similarly, law enforcement officers and emergency responders face everyday exposure to traumatic situations. Humor amongst squads can act as a bonding agent and a buffer against stress, potentially mitigating the effects of long-term strain and trauma. It's a manner for group members to know the absurdity and problems in their work without letting it weigh them down. This form of humor fosters unity and shared knowledge, which is vital for maintaining morale and teamwork in annoying situations.

Beyond character coping, humor profoundly impacts the overall atmosphere of a place of business. A subculture that embraces light-hearted interactions tends to foster a more inclusive environment. It breaks down the invisible barriers among hierarchical tiers, permitting junior groups of workers and senior executives to interact more freely. This democratization of the place of work now not only encourages open communication but also creates a more harmonious painting environment where ideas can drift freely, and collaboration is extra effective.

The Other Five Senses

Companies recognized for their positive place of business cultures often report lower turnover prices, better employee pride, and advanced overall performance. This correlation suggests that humor, far from being only a frivolous addition, is fundamental to fostering an efficient and excellent organizational environment. Employees who chuckle together will likely work correctly, staying stimulated and dedicated to their collective goals.

Leadership involves handling tasks and human beings; humor can be an essential tool in a leader's arsenal. Leaders who hire humor are frequently perceived as extra approachable and relatable, which can drastically decorate their effectiveness. When leaders share amusing or a light-hearted second with their groups, it humanizes them, bridging the gap that titles and roles frequently create.

However, the usage of humor in management requires sensitivity and attention. It ought to be inclusive, never at someone's price, and aligned with the broader values of the organization. When used as it should be, humor can assist leaders in illustrating their factors effectively, diffusing anxiety, and enhancing their messages in memorable ways. It can also serve as a way to inspire teams for the duration of challenging instances, assisting to lighten the mood and boost morale while cut-off dates loom massive or when the team faces setbacks.

Looking at hit organizations and leaders who harness humor, we will see several programs that move past mere stress control. For example, tech giants like Google have long been celebrated for their unconventional painting environments, encompassing playful spaces that inspire creativity and innovation. Here, humor isn't always just about jokes or funny incidents but about fostering a progressive lifestyle where play and paintings intersect seamlessly.

In the culinary enterprise, chefs like Gordon Ramsay exemplify the function of humor even in the most annoying kitchen environments. Despite his reputation for being stern, Ramsay's quick wit and frequently playful banter do more significant than entertain; they cut via the anxiety of the high-stress kitchen, making the demanding situations of culinary excellence more doable and relatable.

In the dynamic and ever-evolving fields of creativity and innovation, the position of humor can't be overstated. Historically, the most innovative spaces—from the supposed tanks of tech giants to the bustling creative flooring of advertising organizations—have identified the utility of a mild-hearted technique in sparking creativity and facilitating groundbreaking thoughts. It's now not honestly about making humans giggle; it is about creating an environment wherein the mental obstacles to unconventional wondering are lowered, and new perspectives can flourish.

Humor works as a catalyst for creativity in several profound ways. Firstly, it lowers the emotional obstacles and the anxiety that could often accompany the stress of innovating. The worry of failure is an excellent impediment in innovative roles in which the expectation is to constantly push obstacles and explore uncharted territories. Humor alleviates some of those pressures, allowing people to take dangers and express thoughts they might, in any other case, maintain to themselves. This is mainly visible in brainstorming sessions where a comic story or humorous commentary can wreck the ice, making room for a more relaxed and open alternative of ideas.

Moreover, humor complements cognitive flexibility—the ability to see connections among apparently unrelated concepts, a center ability in innovative trouble solving. When we snigger, our strain ranges drop, and our frame releases dopamine, beautifying cognitive flexibility. Therefore, individuals in an excellent mood will likely have a broader attention span and extra associative mind, which is essential for creative questioning. This psychological state, regularly called a "relaxed country of alertness," is suitable for producing a wealth of novel ideas.

Implementing humor in an innovative workspace requires more than just an allowance for amusement. It calls for cultivating surroundings where humor is woven into the cloth of the corporation's culture. Leaders play a crucial role in setting this tone. By demonstrating humor, they could signal to their groups that it's ok to be funny and fun with their painting technique. This can include anything from encouraging playful opposition to celebrating failures through funny recaps of "what not to do next time," fostering a culture of mastering and innovation.

In innovative industries like marketing and marketing, humor can now be strategically carried out internally and in the output. Advertisements often use humor to interact with audiences, making messages memorable and shareable. Consider the impact of a viral humorous ad; it is no longer just the product being remembered but the creativity of the advert itself, showcasing the innovativeness of the creators.

Consider a tech company introducing a "Hack Week" wherein employees work on whatever they want. The employer boosts morale and breaks down hierarchical limitations by introducing themes or crew sports that include humorous factors, encouraging free alternatives across departments and seniority tiers. This often results in sudden product ideas or answers that could propel the enterprise forward.

Similarly, in innovative businesses, humor in inner communications and presentations can rework the standard monotony of data overload into an engaging exchange that reinforces retention and encourages creative remarks. The pleasant creative output increases when teams aren't just recipients of facts but engaged contributors.

Despite its many advantages, the usage of humor ought to be navigated cautiously to avoid potential pitfalls. Not all humor is appropriate, and what is funny to one man or woman may be offensive to another. Misjudged humor can not only cause soreness but can also cause tension and battle inside teams, undermining the very creativity its objectives to foster.

To mitigate those risks, fostering inclusive humorousness is essential. This consists of knowledge of the range of the place of job and respecting cultural, social, and private obstacles. A robust method is to encourage humor. This is self-deprecating instead of directed at others, or those goals the industry or corporation lifestyle's quirks, in place of individual traits.

Furthermore, companies must offer education on suitable humor and make it clear that at the same time, while creativity and fun are advocated, respect and inclusivity are paramount. Establishing clear recommendations and channels for feedback on what is or isn't always taken into consideration suitable humor can assist in maintaining delicate stability by encouraging a comfortable, creative environment and keeping a professional and respectful workplace.

The Other Five Senses

In the fabric of human relationships, humor is an important thread, weaving together connections that can withstand the pressures of life's challenges. The significance of possessing a sense of humor transcends mere amusement; it acts as a social lubricant, a coping mechanism, and a cognitive device that complements interpersonal dynamics throughout diverse contexts—from the place of business to family existence and friendships. This discourse delves into why having a sense of humor is critical now for the individual and those around them.

One of humor's most immediate and apparent benefits is its ability to bond humans. Laughter is an established language that transcends cultural and linguistic boundaries, creating an instantaneous sense of togetherness among humans. Sharing a funny story or commentary invites others into a shared space of leisure and light-heartedness. This shared laughter can act as a powerful social glue, growing and strengthening bonds between individuals.

Social psychologists have argued that shared laughter increases emotions of team spirit and trust amongst institution participants. In friendships, humor plays an essential function in developing deeper connections. Friends who can snort together regularly report better levels of pleasure in their relationships. The playful teasing and inner jokes that signify many near friendships help to form a unique bond that is resilient and enduring.

Effective verbal exchange is pivotal in all aspects of existence. Humor complements conversation by breaking down limitations, easing tensions, and making hard conversations more excellent and approachable. In family dynamics, for example, humor can help address touchy subjects and clear up conflicts extra amicably. A mild-hearted remark can exchange the tone of a conversation that might otherwise expand into a controversy, permitting family participants to cope with troubles with much less defensiveness and greater openness.

In expert settings, leaders who use humor are often highly able to interact with their groups. Humorous feedback through presentations or conferences can capture attention and enhance the retention of critical points. Moreover, humor can be an effective tool for leaders to talk about opinions in a manner that is less likely to demoralize personnel, as a substitute, fostering a proactive and effective method of trouble-fixing.

The capacity to giggle during hard times is a full-size aspect of resilience. Humor offers a mental buffer against pressure, anxiety, and melancholy. It allows individuals and people around them to view their conditions more comfortably and balanced. This coping mechanism isn't the simplest beneficial for the individual but also for the ones around them who are probably equally tormented by stressors.

In the stressful circle of relatives or painting environments, one person's potential to lighten her temper will have a ripple effect, enhancing the overall ecosystem and assisting others to manipulate their stress degrees more successfully. This does not imply making light of excellent conditions but rather locating moments of pleasure and laughter that can alleviate and experience desire during hard times.

Groups that laugh collectively regularly assume more excellent creatively together. Humor stimulates mental flexibility, divergent questioning, and the ability to generate novel ideas and answers. In brainstorming periods, whether or not in a company or informal setting, humor can ruin the standard idea styles that would restrict creative wondering. It encourages a playful method to demanding situations, often leading to unconventional answers that won't emerge in more rigid surroundings.

For example, in industries that thrive on innovation, along with advertising and marketing or a place of business tradition that embraces humor is probably extra progressive. This environment lets group individuals feel comfortable and psychologically secure to proportion their most creative thoughts, benefiting the entire group.

Humor contributes considerably to developing supportive and inclusive surroundings. When human beings share fun, it enhances emotions of inclusion and recognition. In any social setting, folks who might feel marginalized can experience extraordinary while humor is used correctly and inclusively.

Humor may be a powerful device in selling mental health cognizance and assistance. By using humor in discussions about mental fitness, the stigma around these subjects may be reduced, making them more handy and much less daunting. This can lead to more recognition and help amongst friends, developing a network wherein people feel supported and understood.

A professional kitchen is often depicted as a battleground in which precision, pace, and perfection are the day's orders. Chefs and kitchen groups of workers face consistent strain from long hours, high expectancies, and the instantaneous comments loop of patron pleasure. In such an environment, the advent of humor may be an essential factor in keeping a balanced environment, assisting in relieving pressure and producing a group nearer.

Leadership inside the kitchen extends beyond culinary competencies and management skills; it additionally involves placing the tone for the place of business subculture.

Chefs who rent humor in their leadership style can make themselves extra approachable, breaking down the barriers that hierarchical structures often erect. When a head chef can shaggy dog story about a mistake or proportion a laugh over a kitchen mishap, it indicators to the relaxation of the group that perfection is a method, now not always an instantaneous result. This approachability encourages open communication, making group participants experience more comfortable discussing issues, sharing ideas, or asking for help.

The announcement, "If you can't stand the heat, get out of the kitchen," underscores the acute environment in which culinary specialists operate. Here, humor acts as a far-wanted release valve for stress. Laughter triggers the release of endorphins, the frame's herbal sense-desirable chemicals. In a kitchen, where bodily and mental strain can speedily collect, a shared joke can help diffuse tension and increase the temper.

Consider the scenario at some stage in an especially busy provider where the pressure stages are high, and the error margin is low. A funny comment or a witty statement can momentarily pierce the bubble of tension, permitting the staff to reset emotionally and awareness with renewed power. This helps preserve a calm demeanor and reinforces a supportive subculture that could face challenges in a more united way.

The Other Five Senses

A group that laughs collectively remains together. Humor is a binding agent that fosters group brotherly love, creating an experience of camaraderie among the body of workers. In kitchens, where diverse groups must work carefully under traumatic conditions, the potential to proportion fun can be an essential part of team-constructing.

This brotherly and sisterly love via humor is frequently cultivated in everyday pre-carrier meetings or workforce food, wherein the ecosystem is more relaxed, and the stakes are momentarily diminished. Here, cooks might proportion funny anecdotes from previous offerings or comic stories about commonplace mishaps. Even though quick, these interactions play a full role in constructing relationships within the team, making the kitchen a cohesive unit that may characteristic efficaciously during high-pressure moments.

In the culinary arts sector, grievance is as steady as the stove's warmth. How one handles grievances can extensively affect personal and expert growth. Humor may be a precious tool in dealing with and getting to know the complaint. A chef who can chuckle at their errors or take complaints in stride, possibly with a witty retort, shows the most effective power and the resilience to study and improve.

Similarly, kitchens frequently face moments of failure—a dish may not come out as intended, or a component is forgotten. A funny angle on such screw-ups could make them much less daunting, turning them into getting-to-know studies instead of discouraging setbacks.

Humor can transforms the kitchen environment into one that is more balanced, resilient, and human. For culinary experts, a sense of humor isn't always just about making each day grind more exciting; it is building a group that can communicate brazenly, innovate freely, and face the pressures of the culinary international with a grin. In essence, humor is not just a coping mechanism but a foundational detail that can increase a kitchen from a place of job to an area of innovative, comfortable collaboration.

In the quick-paced, high-strain surroundings of culinary arts, management requires now not only technical skill and a clear vision but also the capability to manage and inspire various crew. A regularly underestimated humorousness can be an enormous asset for leaders within the kitchen. It can serve as a device for developing a high-quality painting environment and setting up a fair and organized management style. This exploration delves into how culinary leaders can leverage humor to lead their teams efficaciously, hold subject and recognize, and foster an ecosystem conducive to creativity and productivity.

Feedback is an integral part of culinary leadership. The rapid-paced nature of the paintings needs comments to be both immediate and decisive. However, turning in grievance in such a tense environment is a delicate artwork. Leaders ought to ensure that their remarks motivate improvement without demoralizing the group. Here, humor may be a powerful device to melt the edges of critique.

Imagine a situation wherein a dish prepared by a junior chef does not meet the restaurant's standards. A chef ought to bluntly criticize the dish, which would possibly risk demoralizing the cook, or they could inject humor into the feedback, perhaps joking that the dish looks as if it survived meal combat, before stepping into an optimistic critique on the way to better align the presentation with the eating place's excessive standards. This approach makes the remarks more palatable and makes the studying experience attractive and memorable, facilitating a better instructional environment.

The benefits of humor amplify the past, easing anxiety and softening complaints; it is also a powerful tool for boosting team brotherly and sisterly love. In the hierarchical and frequently segmented world of kitchen operations, laughter is an excellent equalizer, breaking down barriers and fostering unity and equality amongst staff. When leaders actively participate in or provoke humor, they seem more approachable and relatable, which is crucial in pulling down hierarchical structures that could often inhibit open verbal exchange and collaboration.

Shared laughter has the electricity to knit team members closer together, creating a place of business culture that values inclusivity and mutual admiration. For instance, while a chef humorously recounts a mistake they made in their early career, it humanizes them and makes it less complicated for junior crew members to narrate to them. This shared vulnerability through humor now not only encourages others to be open about their personal stories but also strengthens the group's bonds. Conversely, this superior cohesion leads to greater powerful collaboration and a supportive knowledge of an environment in which everyone feels valued and empowered to contribute their first-rate.

Implementing humor efficiently requires deep know-how of the team's dynamics and character personalities. Leaders should navigate the first-class line between humor that uplifts and humor that might doubtlessly alienate. Culinary leaders need to domesticate an experience of what's appropriate and what resonates with their specific crew. This would possibly mean avoiding sarcasm, which can be misunderstood without problems, and as a substitute, opting for greater inclusive and mild-hearted humor that celebrates the group's way of life and shared reviews.

Furthermore, timing is fundamental in the use of humor. A comic story that might function as a welcome destroy throughout a gradual prep session can be a distraction at some point for a hectic provider. Leaders must gauge the mood and the tempo of the paintings when deciding on their moments to inject humor.

Fairness and firmness are often considered opposing forces; however, ineffective leadership is complementary. Fairness involves treating all crew individuals with fairness and justice, giving every individual voice the same attention, and recognizing each group member's contributions. Firmness, alternatively, pertains to the unwavering enforcement of regulations and standards and the consistency of a leader in upholding these guidelines.

A chef who masters the stability among those can command recognition and loyalty from their group, which is especially critical in a kitchen environment in which timing, precision, and excellence are demanded continuously. The chef's role then entails a rhythmic dance—understanding while being flexible and standing sturdy, which may appreciably impact the general efficiency and environment of the kitchen.

A common false impression is that humor may undermine authority or lessen the seriousness of team individuals' responsibilities. On the other hand, when used strategically, humor can support excessive standards and expectancies in a memorable and tasty manner. For example, a chef might introduce a playful competition for many kitchen workers to see who can adhere best to presentation requirements or give you the most efficient approach to completing a habitual project. Such competitions, infused with humor and mild-heartedness, not only make the work environment extra fun but also force home the importance of excellence in a non-threatening way.

In the numerous surroundings of an industrial kitchen, appreciation for individual differences and backgrounds is paramount. While used as it should be, humor can play a sizable position in promoting this recognition. Leaders must persuade clear of jokes which could alienate or offend individuals in the group. Instead, focusing on humor that everybody can relate to—including the common challenges and joys in kitchen work—can help enhance a team's harmony and mutual appreciation.

For instance, joking around the "ghost" that seems to misplace the ladles or the "gremlins" that rearrange the spice rack no longer lightens the mood. Still, it subtly emphasizes the commonplace frustrations and shared stories of kitchen paintings. This sort of humor can make crew contributors feel that they're all in the same boat, fostering a supportive and collaborative environment.

Moreover, a pacesetter who laughs at their errors or admits their human moments in a humorous way is a practical example. It shows that despite the high requirements, there is room for human mistakes and studying. This approach no longer most effectively maintains recognition but builds acceptance as true inside the group, as they see their leader as approachable and knowledgeable, encouraging them to try for excellence without the paralyzing worry of failure.

Conflicts in a kitchen are inevitable. When tensions rise, a frontrunner's use of humor may be a quick and effective tool for de-escalation. A light-hearted remark or a humorous commentary can assist in defusing anger and open the door for more excellent rational communication. It's essential, however, that this humor is not used to push aside the seriousness of the conflict but rather to create a space in which answers can be mentioned brazenly and constructively.

For instance, throughout a heated argument about an appropriate recipe preparation, a pacesetter would possibly interject with a funny observation about how each party fiercely protects their "culinary youngsters." This can shift the tone from aggressive to one wherein every birthday celebration can chuckle, step again, and look at the state of affairs with a new attitude, perhaps leading to a compromise or a new revolutionary technique that combines each strategy.

In the excessive-stakes, excessive-pressure global of culinary arts, wherein the heat of the kitchen can each forge and fracture groups, the implementation of humor by using leaders' wishes to be as strategic and considerate as their maximum complex recipes. The blessings of humor in management—improving morale, improving communique, and easing strain—are nicely documented. Still, the execution of humor must be nuanced, reflecting a deep understanding of the crew's dynamics, cultural backgrounds, and delivery timing. This exploration delves into the complexities of efficiently implementing humor in culinary leadership, specializing in expertise in the target audience, gaining knowledge of the timing, and leading by example.

The Other Five Senses

The foundational step in efficaciously enforcing humor is understanding the target audience very well—the kitchen body of workers. Culinary teams typically comprise people from diverse cultural backgrounds, each bringing precise views and sensitivities. What is considered humorous in a single way of life can be visible as offensive or beside the point in every other. Therefore, a chef or a culinary chief has to first invest time in getting to know their group contributors individually and professionally.

Understanding your audience entails more than simply knowing their cultural backgrounds; it also includes their personalities, strain thresholds, and daily reviews within the kitchen. For instance, a comic story that might be well-received after a successful career might not be suitable inside the center of a disturbing dinner rush. Chefs need to be attuned to the moods and emotions of their crew participants, gauging while they're open to humor and when they could want a more extraordinary, honest form of assistance.

Moreover, leaders should be aware of the man or woman demanding situations that group members may face. A young apprentice might be extra sensitive to jokes about errors, fearing they replicate doubts about their talents. At the same time, a pro sous chef would possibly welcome such jokes as a signal of camaraderie and attractiveness. Thus, a vital element of the effective use of humor is ensuring it is inclusive, builds individuals up, and reinforces their value to the team rather than alienating every person or exacerbating current pressures.

In comedy, timing is regularly referred to as essential to fulfilling a shaggy dog story. In the context of culinary leadership, the timing of humor is as vital, if now not extra. Leaders must be adept at studying the room and choosing moments when humor will relieve anxiety in preference to add to it. The rapid-paced nature of kitchen paintings, with its inherent highs and lows, calls for a leader to quickly verify conditions and decide the most opportune moments to inject humor.

For instance, for the duration of a debrief after an especially hard provider, a leader could use humor to lighten the temper and transition the crew from a high-stress mindset to a more reflective and relaxed kingdom wherein they can examine from experience. Alternatively, humor can be used preemptively, earlier than a regarded annoying occasion like a tremendous feast or a go-to from a famous critic, to ease anxiety and foster a spirit of teamwork.

However, timing in humor is not just about when to tell a funny story but also about the extreme. Leaders ought to stabilize their use of humor with identical displays of professionalism and focus, ensuring that their team knows the importance of their roles and duties. This balance preserves admiration and credibility, ensuring that humor no longer undermines a frontrunner's effectiveness.

Perhaps the most effective way to ensure the proper use of humor within a group is for leaders to model it themselves. Leaders set the requirements and expectancies for anybody else by demonstrating what they consider appropriate humor. This method entails using self-deprecating humor or performing on the not-unusual reports and challenges confronted by the crew instead of making jokes on the fee of character crew participants.

Leading by using instance and manner, showing how to react to humor. Leaders need to be gracious while on the receiving end of jokes, demonstrating how to take humor in stride and recognize it as part of the crew's interaction. This conduct encourages a secure and respectful environment where humor is used as a tool for bonding instead of as a weapon.

Additionally, by using humor judiciously, leaders train their groups that while humor is valued, it is not the sole tool for conversation or leadership. They display that there are times for fun and seriousness, helping crew contributors expand their sense of humor while it's appropriate and detracts from the project to hand.

Implementing humor successfully in culinary management is a complex, however rewarding approach. It requires deep expertise of the various personalities that make up the team, an impeccable timing experience to ensure that humor provides price rather than a distraction, and a capability to steer by example. When executed successfully, humor complements the team's functioning and enriches the painting environment, making the extreme international culinary arts a more exciting and cohesive space. For leaders inclined to spend money on gaining knowledge of the way to use humor correctly, the payoff may be huge, mainly for extra resilient, communicative, and influential groups.

My Final Thoughts

What a ride these past six chapters have been! My hope is that this work has now brought an awareness of the many honorable qualities that come with the vocation of chef.

So many times through the years, I have made an appearance at events and a person would ask a question on how chefs do certain tasks. And I would have an explanation that would often amaze them, but for me because I dedicated my whole life to my craft the reply I gave would come as second nature.

Mastering cooking techniques and knife skills are very important parts of the mechanics of cooking, but as you now have read to be a chef requires far more.

As a little kid, growing up in an Italian house, food played an important role in my professional decisions. As a portion of this book articulates many factors play into our food choices. The flavors and textures we favor over others, but when I think of food as a generalized topic the word association for me is simple – *"happiness"*. When I am in the kitchen of a restaurant, a personal chef client, on stage at a food show in front of an audience, a food hall doing catering I want the receiving party to experience the same sense of happiness that I associate food with my entire life, but what a journey those ingredients had to take and the team effort required to get food into the dining room.

In a professional sense of chef to employee, my job is to have the team understand that their job is more than a job. For front-of-the-house employees, it is more than pressing buttons on a point-of-sale

The Other Five Senses

computer screen. It's my job to convey to them like everyone in the entire restaurant that their jobs are a *craft*. It's a craft to be an excellent bartender or waitperson; it's a craft to be an excellent line cook and prep person. The act of repetition is required to make employees get closer and closer to mastering their skills. Furthermore, the thought of a person's job as a craft goes beyond the culinary arts. Career paths like being a lawyer, a teacher, or a doctor should share the same mentality of craft fullness. Think of it this way, the difference between an excellent lawyer, teacher, and doctor and a bad one is that most likely the excellent ones were around other experienced lawyers, teachers, and doctors who allowed them to watch them practice the craft. Once a person passes the bar, in theory, they are an attorney, but the truth is they are a person who went to school, sat and took a test, and passed but to sit in the back of a courtroom to see other attorneys put their craft into action is what will make their development priceless.

Chefs make our employees better; we transform them by expanding their working knowledge of what we place on our menus. As the person responsible for what's on the menu I never wrote a menu in which employees felt they knew everything on it. Many times I have made familiar food, but never made them the same ways or plated them the same, which they are probably accustomed to. There was always something that needed to be learned. This made employees see the same Caesar salad that they saw a million times before in a new way with a new presentation and in addition does the same for the client.

In conclusion, I hope that this work can be a real look into the lives, qualities and demands that chefs such as myself need to meet and that I *always* obtained by developing these *other five senses*.

Working on ourselves and being our personal and professional best allows us to have these same qualities and senses develop in those around us.

www.ingramcontent.com/pod-product-compliance
Lightning Source LLC
Chambersburg PA
CBHW071812160426
43209CB00032B/1935/J